LEAVE
—WITH—
LOVE

A SPIRITUAL GUIDE

LEAVE
—WITH—
LOVE

FINDING PEACE, SELF-LOVE,
AND COMPASSION WHEN
LEAVING RELATIONSHIPS

ATHENA ALLREAD

SEASIDE ⚓ SHAMAN
ATHENA ALLREAD

ISBN: 978-0-578-54200-3

Cover Photography: Meghan LaPrairie Photography
Cover Design & Interior Layout: Byzantium Sky Press

This book is dedicated to all of my teachers.

To Mommy: for teaching me from heaven that relationships never truly end. For sharing the magic of the afterlife
with me. For loving me unconditionally.

To my babies Kai, Wolf and Lark: for teaching me grace.

To Forest: The first love of my life. The inspiration for
this book. For teaching me firsthand many of the lessons
included in this book. May we walk forward with love
through many more lives and learning experiences.

And to each of my clients: for trusting me as your guide
through the spirit worlds, for sharing your stories with
such trust and for teaching me about the many facets of
relationship.

CONTENTS

INTRODUCTION   i

CHAPTER 1   **1**
truth & illusions

CHAPTER 2   **21**
understanding soul relationships

CHAPTER 3   **37**
metamorphosis

CHAPTER 4   **43**
karma & relationship roles

CHAPTER 5   **55**
the seven demons of change

CHAPTER 6   **81**
leaving

CHAPTER 7   **99**
visions of a better future

CHAPTER 8   **111**
how to leave

CHAPTER 9   **127**
surrender & rebirth: the dark night of the soul

CHAPTER 10   **149**
alone-ness & self-realization

CHAPTER 11   **167**
leaving with love

GLOSSARY   **175**

ABOUT THE AUTHOR   **177**

INTRODUCTION

REGARDLESS of the parties in a relationship (parent-child, brother-sister, husband-wife, teacher-student, donor-recipient, employer-employee, or friend-friend), we've come here to earth to share many different experiences in love and relating to others... and when the time comes to leave these relationships, we are left with the arduous task of learning how to *Leave with Love*. This book is my attempt to guide you in doing so.

Leave with Love is a gentle command from Spirit, that great collective of the Divine and your own Higher Self, which asks you to trust in your inside guidance and know that in following the wisdom of the heart, you will be safe and loved. This book is meant to be a loving and supportive companion to you or your loved one through relationship transitions. No matter which end of the transition you are on, whether you are on the giving or the receiving end of a release, this book will provide you with tools for softening into the transition.

As you are in touch with your own Divine nature, you will continue to love this other person (or place or group). To unconditionally love others is the way of divinity and if you are in touch with your Self as a Divine being, then you will always be extending out love. It will be painful at times, and exhilarating at other times, however if you can find and stand firm in your Self, you will not lose your Self to the pain as it moves through. This pain is a symbol of movement. The comings and goings of energy of your past. Memories will surface. Observe them with love and gratitude and peace and know that each of these memories was a deep and beautiful learning experience and stepping stone for your soul.

Know that the pain of this release is not permanent. **Surrender** to the unknown of when you will be reunited with your beloved and trust that you will. It may be in this lifetime and it may be in the next; but you *will* be reunited. You *will* have new opportunities to share love and growth and to learn from one another. But for now surrender to the unknown. If you're coming into this book in excruciating pain, please jump ahead to Chapter Nine - Surrender & Rebirth. This book can be explored as you feel guided, it is not required to be read from front to back as our journeys in healing are not always linear.

I wish you much peace, healing and clarity on your journey back home to your Self.

1

TRUTH & ILLUSIONS

Relationships Never Truly End

 We may meet again later in life or we may
not meet again until another lifetime, but
we will most certainly meet again.
ATHENA ALLREAD

We leave our homes at the start of the new day, and we return.
Sometimes we leave for extended trips, sometimes we return within minutes. Other times we leave our homes in the pursuit of a
new home. But we always return home. Home is: our resting place,
our place of Oneness with ourselves, our place with loved ones or
with the Divine. If we can begin to view every person we are in a
relationship with as an extension of home, then we can leave a relationship with a dear friend for six months or six years, and return
back 'home' to that special friendship after all of this time apart.
We can 'lose' a loved one to the Spirit world and meet times again
in the dream realm and again when we join them in heaven.

Relationships don't end. They pause. They take breaks. They
change form.

The belief that they end is an illusion. What if in this moment
we could soften into a truth that relationships never end? An understanding that we may meet again later in life or we may not
meet again until another lifetime, but we will most certainly meet
again. We leave and part ways heading in different directions for
various reasons, and we meet again.

If we can open up to the possibility or notion that our relationships never truly end, than within the pain of separation, we can find acceptance and Love.

You will carry with you the lessons, memories and experiences gained in each relationship. The markings of time and space shared with this person. At the end of this chapter is an exercise in gratitude. I encourage you to sit down and review these markings of time and space shared with whomever is at the other side of this relationship transition, and hold gratitude.

But don't get me wrong...

Leaving relationships is hard. It HURTS! I have found that it is much more difficult to *Leave with Love* and to have trust and faith in the potential for growth and freedom that follows. When we lack this faith, we often remain in expired relationships until a (often uncomfortable) catalytic circumstance forces us into change. These catalytic circumstances can all have much more dire consequences, leaving years of hurt, guilt and regret on both sides.

Finding the Beauty in Impermanence

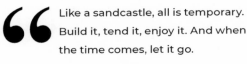

Like a sandcastle, all is temporary.
Build it, tend it, enjoy it. And when
the time comes, let it go.

JACK KORNFIELD

I FIRST came to accept impermanence through the lens of art and later in my studies of Buddhism. The concept of impermanence simply holds that *everything* in existence comes into being and dissolves. Nothing lasts, and everything decays. As a fine artist and painter I was rigid, attached to the outcome of my work. I feared mistakes and perceived failure with the slightest error. I would plan my paintings in my mind, spend hours outlining them in pencil before ever actually putting the brush to paper, and I would spend even more hours meticulously painting and blending tones and edges in my work. Eventually I abandoned color and the majority of my work was black and white, where my focus was strictly on the contrast between the two, and on using the limitations of lack of color to illustrate contour and spatial relationships. It was at freshman orientation at university that I attended a talk about the architecture program and found a comfortable home for my obsessive attention to detail and need for precision. After many years of working within the strict confines in architecture, I yearned for more freedom of expression. I desired to break out of my rigidity. Synchronously I ran into an artist friend of mine and in conversation she made mention of a concept she called 'sand-castle art'. She shared that when she approached art with the desire to create freely, she treated it as a sandcastle. She would treat it as if she knew and expected that eventually the tide would pull it out to sea. The art would then be an offering to the sea. When we spend hours on the beach as children or with our children, we sit together building beautiful structures, creating stories togeth-er, creating freely without any attachment because we know at the end of the day our castle will be swept to sea. We take pictures, we marvel at our work, we savor the moment. We don't fear losing our sandcastle because we *know* we will lose our sandcastle, and so we put our all into it fearlessly.

I loved this idea and the energy of creative fearlessness. I latched on and tried to let go of my own rigidity. I would do my best in whatever I was working at, holding onto my desire to build some-thing amazing, but releasing attachment to the outcome. *(It wasn't until deep into my shamanic work that I thought to apply this concept to relationships.)* What if we could fearlessly play, create and build beautiful relationships with others without attachment... know-ing that at some point these relationships too, would get washed away by the tide?

The Illusion of Comfort

 The lust for comfort, that stealthy thing
that enters the house as a guest, and then
becomes a host and then a master.

KHALIL GIBRAN

THERE is a spark that exists within us that desires for security
and stability. We want to live long healthy lives and we want our
loved ones to live long healthy lives. We seek (and if lucky, we find)
security and stability through the comfort provided by people,
places and sources outside of ourselves.

I define a comfortable relationship as a relationship that is in
a state of rest and homeostasis, a state of relative equilibrium. A
comfortable relationship can vary from person to person. We can
be at rest under positive conditions, but we can also find ourselves
at rest in a condition of pain if we've become accustomed to it.
For one person a comfortable relationship could be a relationship
you've been in for many many years and you feel at rest, at ease,
and don't feel the need for anything more. For another, a comfortable relationship could be a relationship with characteristics that
rests within the limits of everything that person has ever known...
Such as in the case of a man who has been with his partner for
many years and has his basic needs for companionship met, but
has some unmet needs for adventure, spiritual depth and inspiration. Or the woman who has only ever known abusive men and

thus feels comfortable in relationships with abusive men. Both of these individuals are comfortable but being summoned by Spirit to open up to greater things on offer. I name comfort as an illusion here because it can function like a veil brought down over our eyes to conceal the possibilities and potentialities for greater things.

When we linger in this resting state too long, our dreams and desires begin to pass us by. We forget the things that we loved prior to this relationship, we postpone our desires and sometimes even abort our original missions. Comfort can hold us back from fulfilling our purpose.

When comfort is lost we get uncomfortable. It is in these moments of discomfort we 'wake up' and begin to question whether we were living a lie, whether we can trust our own judgements, whether everything that we thought we knew was in fact an illusion. The discomfort that comes as we near the gateways of change is a catalyst propelling us into growth and expansion.

We can find balance in the oscillation between comfort and discomfort by observing the rhythm between the two. Examining where our source of comfort lies and where our source of discomfort stems. Observe the triggers. In a literal sense, the emotions and sensations of our bodies are great teachers of how we navigate the space between comfort and discomfort. For example, womens bodies in particular carry internal 'sensors' of change. We sync up to the moon with our menstrual cycles and when we are aware, we can sense the coming cycle via triggers of emotion and sensation within the body. Within our full four-week cycle, we experience three weeks of comfort or 'normality' and one week of emotional and physical 'discomfort'. During that period of discomfort, our bodies, minds and spirits need to rest and allow the changes taking place within to pass. Our relationships are quite the same in that the moods of the relationship will ebb and "flow" with the moons. Over the course of a month, a year, a Venus orbit, a Saturn return, or other cycle... and like a menstrual cycle, your relationships will experience "periods" of 'comfort' and periods of 'discomfort'.

Knowing when the relationship is operating outside the zone of tolerable discomfort is critical for making the decision to leave. *(See the exercise at the end of this section for guidance on determining where you fall on the scale of tolerable discomfort).* Think of a headache and a migraine. A headache at times can be tolerable, maybe caused by lack of water or food and some muscular tension, while a migraine is a severe, unbearable, debilitating neurological disorder. Is your relationship discomfort a headache... Or a migraine?

The severity of discomfort can be an indicator for what level of change your relationship would benefit from. Change might not necessarily be leaving a relationship for good, it may mean leaving the relationship as it was behind and building a new one. What is the difference between leaving a relationship and building a new one? The difference is in your choice to stay with the same person, group or organization and make a change or to choose to dissolve your roles as they were. For a couple, they could decide to no longer be 'boyfriend' and 'girlfriend' but to enter into a new relationship as friends. A supervisor could decide to end an employees relationship as boss and subordinate and make them a partner. Change can be very positive and beneficial to both parties.

I see many couples who love each other very much and unintentionally inhibit one another from moving toward their dreams out of fear and the perceived threat to their stability- the wife that prohibits her husband from retiring early for fear of lack, the husband that prohibits his wife from taking that leap of faith into her passion, the girlfriend that prohibits the boyfriend from traveling for fear of loss, or the employer that prohibits the employee from taking that precious time off for fear of falling behind. Our personal desires for comfort and stability often times hold ourselves and our loved ones back under the illusions of our own fears.

9

Fear can manifest as a reluctance to look at, to see what we don't understand or believe to be possible. We can choose to remain comfortable and resist change out of fear, we can choose to allow the fears of our loved ones to prohibit us from growth and expansion, or we can choose to learn, grow and fulfill our dreams and desires. It is your free will choice.

Have gratitude for your periods of comfort. If you'd like to remain there, *stay*! If you're ready to break out of the comfort zone... *keep reading!*

1.01 Exercise

INTENTION: Review your comfort level in a relationship

ACTION: Examine your relationship with your Self, your town, your family, partner. Are you feeling in alignment with your dreams? If not, begin to meditate on your dreams, where your sense of purpose lies and how your relationship(s) can support you in aligning with it.

Examining our sources of comfort and where our sources of discomfort stem from. Usually our sources of discomfort present as fears, and once we can review those fears, we can release ourselves from them and mobilize forward. List all of the fears of your own *and* the fears of anyone else in your life that are prohibiting you from moving forward with your dreams. Begin to move through the list and label each fear on a scale of 1-5, 1 being not scary at all and 5 being frightening. This is your measure of tolerable to intolerable discomfort, (1) being tolerable and (5) being intolerable.

EFFECT: Once you've determined the fears that instill intolerable discomfort in you, take a moment to sit quietly and meditate and allow for inspirations and guidance to come through on how you can carefully navigate your way toward your dreams. You will likely be guided in baby steps forward, releasing tiny behaviors or habits or patterns of thinking. With your full faith, Spirit will guide you forward safely.

The Illusion of Rejection

 In these moments of complete loss of
contact and lack of response, we feel
robbed of a potential future.

ATHENA ALLREAD

You weren't the chosen one. You were dismissed, refused, released.
You were not chosen because you didn't meet or measure up to the
requirements of someone else and so you begin to question *your*
value.

Regardless of which side of the perceived 'rejection' you are on,
the lending or the receiving, this can be a painful dealing. My client Lana came to me after a painful separation from her husband,
in which he'd decided to leave her for another woman. Although
relationships are usually unraveling long before the catalytic ex-
tramarital relationship ensues, we are still left with the bitter sensation of feeling rejected. Lana and I worked together through
each of the painful emotions that followed the perceived rejection. Lana's spirit guides and angels provided insights into what
her partner was experiencing, helping her to see through his eyes,
shared potential outcomes for her relationship with her partner,
and most importantly helped her to see the beauty within her
Self. All of which helped to soften into the pain of the rejection
itself. After my own experiences in rejection, and years of watching those I love experience it, I sat down with Spirit and asked the

question: What is rejection?

The answer that I heard back: The belief in rejection of *the person* is an illusion... the rejection is of *the offering*. It is an unwillingness to accept an offer. A denial of an offering. *You* are not being rejected, *your offering* is being rejected.

Imagine yourself walking into a beautiful gem shop and find the seller presenting you with a beautiful emerald ring. You pick it up, examine it, and contemplate purchasing it. You look at the price tag and decide that it's more than you can afford. You politely decline the sellers offer. You *reject* their offering.

Rejection is an illusion which can be created by either party, the lender or the recipient of the perceived 'rejection'. When you feel rejected, you are under a false vision of your Self as a product or entity that can be denied. *You* cannot be rejected but your offering can be. Your work is to practice non-attachment to the expectation that *your offering* will be accepted. Extend your offerings out without fear. If you are seeking exchange and wanting to make an offering and receive something in return, set your terms for the exchange. Decline offers that don't align with your terms. Don't abandon your terms for fear of another not accepting them. You have a valuable offering.

I used to envy the people who seem to so easily brush off 'rejection' and keep moving forward. What is their secret!?

The secret is this: People that brush off rejection so easily are able to do so because they know their own value. They are excellent negotiators. They approach a potential partnership as an opportunity for a new exchange. They enter knowing their value, they exit knowing their value. They *do not* compromise or exit questioning their value.

Ladies, let's say you spot a gorgeous man at the bar. You feel a magnetic attraction pulsating between the two of you and anxiously wait for him to come and talk to you. You're a bit old fashioned and like for the man to be the initiator so you keep waiting. You lock eyes for an extended moment but then he glances around, spots another woman, and moves over and begins chatting her up. Disappointed that he didn't make his way to you, you begin to feel overcome with the weight of rejection. You question why. For many women, our first instinct is to begin to judge ourselves. The stream of consciousness of self-doubts... Is it my hair, my shoes, is my dress not sexy enough, is my dress too sexy? Is it because I'm ethnic or because I have curly hair? I'm not good enough for him. I'm not worthy of his attention. Maybe. Maybe not. What's happened is this man has entered the bar, a marketplace for new relationships, and he's entered with a clear idea of what he has to offer and what he's looking for in exchange. Maybe you're not it. And that's okay. But have you entered with a clear idea of what you are looking for? If so, do you believe he is your only option? In your battle against those feelings of rejection, it's important to know your value.

When relationships end, it is quite common that one party experience some sensation of rejection. Following the belief of rejection, the doorway to those Seven Demons of Transition (Chapter Five) is opened. Shame, Hurt, Anger, Resentment all make their way in. We can do our best to keep the door to these demons shut by cutting through the illusion and recognizing our own value. And through acceptance giving permission for others to recognize their value and to set their own costs and standards within this marketplace of love.

Rejection is especially common in today's era of online dating and social media centered relationships. In online dating I hear many accounts of men and women who've seemingly met great potential partners only to hear nothing from them after a few conversations. I myself was in a passionate relationship with a man for eight weeks only to have him completely 'ghost' out of the blue one day. No call, no text, no email... nothing. The term "ghosting" refers to a situation where one person ceases communication with the other with no explanation. In 2016 dating site Plenty of Fish shared findings that 78% of single Millennials (people on the site between the ages of 18 and 33) have been "ghosted" at least once.

In these moments of complete loss of contact and lack of response, we feel robbed of a potential future. We opened up, we pursued, we shared, and we allowed ourselves to be vulnerable even if only for a minute... We gave a sample of our valuable goods. And the buyer decided to walk.

This is extremely painful yet if we can honor the buyers decision to walk, remember our value and commit to selling our goods for what they are worth... A worthy buyer WILL come along.

1.02 Exercise

INTENTION: Release feelings of rejection from a specific person

ACTION: Write a letter directly to someone who has initiated feelings of rejection for you. This doesn't have to be someone you had romantic interest in, this could be a teacher, a former employer, a parent... Anyone who once spurred feelings of rejection within you. Think about what you were offering to them, was it love? money? service? Imagine yourself going back to the moment they declined your offer and giving them permission to maintain *their* needs and desires and to know what *they* were ready or willing to trade. Compassionately forgive them for not choosing your offering. Thank them for the opportunity to hold out for the right buyer for your offering..

EFFECT: With compassionately reviewing the bird's-eye view of a moment of perceived rejection and giving others permission to maintain their needs and desires, you in turn give yourself permission to maintain your own needs and desires. You release the negative weighted feelings of rejection and allow for a sense of lightness to move in and for Spirit to support you in attracting in the 'right buyer' for your offering.

1.03 Exercise

INTENTION: Reassess your value

ACTION: In your journal, computer or on a separate sheet of paper, create a sell sheet and set your selling price. Imagine yourself to be like the greatest show horse. Find the most incredible photo of yourself—the photo that makes you think "DAMN!" Print it onto a sheet of paper. Write up a beautiful profile articulating every beautiful aspect of yourself; including scars, moles, birthmarks and tattoos. Describe a subtle quality about yourself, like the way that you walk. List all of your strengths. List all of the places you've been or where you'd like to go. How you like to eat. What you like to wear. How you work out (or don't). Your favorite dance moves or music to listen to. Write anything that makes you unique and valuable.

Next, determine your target market.

This part can be done when you are ready for a new relationship or when you would like to re-evaluate your values to get clear on what you need and desire in an existing relationship. * If you are not ready for a new relationship, you may decide to revisit this exercise months down the line and that's okay.

When you are ready, sit and assess who your target market is. Write down everything that comes to mind in what type of buyer you would like to attract, whether that be for work, love, client or other.

Finally, write your asking price. Your asking price is whatever it is that you are asking for from this new or existing relationship.

What are you asking for? If your reviewing a love interest perhaps you're asking for a long term arrangement, acceptance, a hiking partner, affection, devotion and if it's an employer maybe you're asking for a set salary, flexible hours, health benefits, creative freedom... Write down what you want, no limitations.

EFFECT: After reassessing your value, determining your target market and your asking price, you will limit yourself from future exposure to feelings of rejection. You will be more aware of who you are seeking and quickly able to let go when your terms cannot be met. This is a practice and won't always be easy, there will be times when you question or doubt your value, but when you do, come back to your 'sell sheet' and remember how worthy you are!

The Illusion of Loss

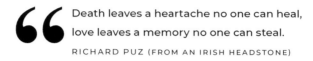

> Death leaves a heartache no one can heal,
> love leaves a memory no one can steal.
>
> RICHARD PUZ (FROM AN IRISH HEADSTONE)

ON Christmas night, after the children were tucked in bed, with family circled around her hospice bed holding hands, my Mommy took her last breaths and departed.

I was staying in a hotel three traffic lights from the hospice center. While giving my son Wolf a bath, I had a feeling to call and check in, even though I'd only been gone an hour. My cousin said to me in a low voice "her breathing has changed, you may want to get back here..." I grabbed my things and ran out of the hotel. Just as I was running out the door I caught a glimpse of a figure in my left peripheral view. I turned to see a heavier set woman of color with a walker lugging two huge suitcases up the hill toward the hotel entrance. I could tell she needed help. I looked back at my van and back at the woman and then up to the sky and thought *"God will forgive me if I don't help her..."* And yet some powerful force pulled me over to help that woman smiling her way up that hill this cold Christmas night. "Are you alone?" I asked her. "Yes, but I am blessed." she responded. I helped her carry her bags up the hill. Once we reached the top, she thanked me for helping her and I knew in that moment that my Mommy had passed on. I knew that she would also be traveling alone... but that she too would be blessed. I knew that in some way, this angel had stepped into the night to support me through what would be my most painful loss.

The greatest pain and anger I've experienced in my life occurred the night my mom passed. That Christmas night she left for heaven, I was overcome with anger and rage. I declared that there must not be a God and finding a piece of torn paper in my hotel room I wrote "What kind of God would allow such a beautiful loving angel to suffer so?!"

The next day riding in the car I was suddenly hit with an excruciating pain in my chest. I was sure that it was a heart attack and started to have difficulty breathing. I told my husband that we needed to get to the hospital. I felt numb in my limbs. I consciously knew that he was aware of the likelihood that grief had overtaken me and yet the pain was very real and my panic persisted... He remained calm and coached me through breathing. After what felt like eternity (but was likely only eight minutes) I was able to breathe my way back down and soften into the pain.

For days, I walked in a static-y haze of pain and numbness. The cold wintry day of her funeral, I gazed up at the sky. The sun shine like I'd never seen it in my life. I knew that she was there looking down at me, and I knew that she was now reunited with God. In that moment God spoke to me like never before and answered that question I'd been sitting with for days, "Suffering moves us." With that three word answer I was flooded with understanding. I understood that in my mother's suffering, she had affected so many others like a ripple effect. Friends, family, neighbors moved into caregiver mode, compassion poured in and out from all corners and a majestic fountain of love. We were all introduced to new ways of thinking, we searched for new ways of eating, new ways of healing, new ways of connecting and sharing love. Some of us who hadn't spoken in years selflessly stepped forward to embrace one another as we lay by her bedside. It was painful. But it was beautiful.

Nearly nine months after her passing, I found myself ill with a terrible gastrointestinal condition. I was vomiting daily, losing weight and in extreme pain. In and out of various doctors' offices for months, undergoing invasive testing, and nothing working. Eventually when I was desperate for relief and willing to try anything. I called the local shaman. I was sure it was some form of undiagnosed cancer, having just lost my mom to colon cancer. I went to this shaman in tears, feeling completely defeated and hopeless. And after 30 minutes of waving her hands over my body and shaking my arms and torso, she turned me over and asked "What are you sad about?"

"I lost my Mom..." I replied in barely a whisper.

"Your mom's not lost, she's right here!" the Shaman proclaimed and preceded to tell me things about my mother that no stranger could have possibly known. My mother was there by my side. "You need to grieve" She said to me. "If you don't, it WILL become cancer."

I went home that night and tossed up the question "How do I grieve?" and I heard an answer back from somewhere in my own mind... "Write letters to your mom." And so that first night of my healing journey, I wrote my first letter to my Mom.

I woke up the next day healed.

Not long after, my mom came to me in a vision and shared with me her experience crossing over to the other side. She showed me the bliss of the experience and of the afterlife. My fear of death completely dissolved. I finally understood that death was not the end. After several months of pain and illness, I was seemingly miraculously healed. The false belief that my mom was lost, was gone.

After my personal healing experience and the journey that followed, I've come to work comfortably with the Spirit world every single day and I've come to see and believe that the perception of 'loss' is an illusion. Our loved ones that cross out of this life and into the next, are always by our sides. They are never lost for good. When we lose a husband, wife, sibling, child, or employee to circumstances beyond our control, we have never truly 'lost' them. We always hold the ability to see and speak directly to their soul.

1.04 Exercise

INTENTION: To soften the pain of perceived loss.

ACTION: In a space where you feel safe for an emotional release, sit with a journal or loose paper for writing. *Note: Exercises like this are best done just before bed as it allows for greater clarity and relief to come in the dreams.* Think of the person that you believe you've lost holding a picture of them in your mind and allowing for ALL of the thoughts and feelings bubbling to come up to the surface. In your journal begin to unpack these thoughts and feelings as they come. Let this person know how you're doing. If you're feeling terrible, let them know. Be honest, don't lie. If you feel you need clarity on anything, *just ask*. Share whatever you desire to of your current world, proud moments and accomplishments, dreams. Speak directly to their soul.

EFFECT: Because the heart does break and close after perceived loss, this work of communicating on the soul level can be extremely effective in healing and opening your heart back up. With an open heart you are more receptive to seeing, hearing, feeling the signs of reassurance from above that your loved one is always with you. Watch for those signs!

2

UNDERSTANDING SOUL RELATIONSHIPS

Understanding Soul Relationships

 The meeting of two personalities is like
the contact of two chemical substances: if
there is any reaction, both are
transformed.

CARL GUSTAV JUNG

We come here to Earth, in this human form to experience love in
all facets. We come to experience unconditional love, unrequited
love, agape love, familial love, friendship love, self-love, romantic
love, passionate love and the many facets of love.

I believe that if you can even slightly understand the vastness
of human life and the purpose of the human experience. You can
more easily navigate and heal the many relationships that flow in
and out of your life. You can welcome them for all of the beautiful lessons that they bring, and you can heal the pain of separation
through gratitude for those lessons.

Each day, from the moment we wake, we are interacting and relating in so many varied ways with so many varied types of relationships. If we look at each relationship within and around our
lives as an agreement with another soul to help us to experience
and learn these many facets of love, we can thank each soul for
their teaching, step further into our Divine self and cherish each
relationship with love.

We've made agreements with these souls to share in specific
experiences and lessons. Attraction is our souls compass guiding

us to move forward (or not) with people we meet along our path. Our soul recognizes qualities within another person or organization that are in alignment with our own. Many of our initial encounters with soul mates and soul family are pre-destined, already laid out before we've even come into this life. Instinctually, at that initial encounter or 'reunion' with a familiar soul our souls know that a new teacher has stepped onto the platform.

I love sharing the story of how I met my best friend Katie and how we've been inseparable since that first reunion. Her husband had set us up on a blind library date with our toddlers. Having never seen a picture or met this woman, when I first laid eyes on her I knew her. I immediately felt her as a sister and it was mutual and we saw each other nearly every day in those first months. Early in our friendship, our lives paralleled in miraculous ways, we both conceived our third child within months of one another, bringing us to have all three children of the same age. We supported one another through the trials of pregnancy, motherhood, career leaps, relationship troubles and living in a new town. There was a great ease in being with one another. It was also Divine timing that she came into my life just as I was losing my mother. As my best friend 'mommy' made her transition up into heaven, this loving Universe gave me a new best friend to fill that wide open gaping hole left behind in my heart. Katie, along with my daughter Lark, filled me up in ways I didn't know I needed and helped me to heal through the grieving process. All three of these women are **soul mates** in my life.

Types of Soul Relationships

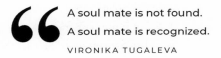

A soul mate is not found.
A soul mate is recognized.
VIRONIKA TUGALEVA

Soul mate encounters can be characterized by an instinctive know-ing and feelings of safety and security. Comfort and ease. Some believe that you can and will have many soulmates along your life path, lovingly changing hands at pivotal moments in time. When you come across a soulmate on your path, you meet them with a sense of familiarity or recognition. They can be a love partner, dear friend, family... Even uncles and aunts, cousins, parents, children and siblings can be soulmates who you share a deep soul connec-tion. You've known them in other lifetimes and your soul imme-diately recognizes that warm connection, often before your con-sciousness does. Our reunions in this lifetime are synchronous and filled with magic and are usually predestined from before the moment of birth. Soulmates can act as contracted earth angels in our lives, here to guide, protect, love and help us to heal through our most difficult times. They are some of our greatest teachers.

A romantic soulmate differs from a twin flame in that it is a saf-er dwelling place for the heart to rest. It is not marked by the roll-ercoaster of emotions and separation; and in contrast to the twin flame that markedly shows up at an unexpected moment in time, a soulmate shows up when conditions are ripe for a new relationship to grow. The grounds have been cleared, other relationships have likely been left behind to create the space for the soulmate to land... no matter how recently. A key point is that a soul mate connection with the opposite sex is not necessarily defined by a romantic connection nor is there a requirement for commitment. We have free will and can choose what degree of relating and intimacy we desire with another. We can choose to define or not define our relationships. Most importantly, we can choose when we leave these relationships.

Many soulmates will be in our lives for extended periods if not for as long as both parties are living and crossing paths. Some soulmates will come in for a particular segment of our lives, for example during school years, during a work contracting period, during a divorce or loss or new move. During these times they will be a loving guide and support for us.

twin flames - catalysts

"How many times did we pass each other before we met? If only
I'd known... I would have searched for you endlessly. If only
I'd found you before it was already too late."
RANATA SUZUKI

THERE'S that old dreamy ideal of a soul mate... that person you've waited for all your life, "the One" who comes in and sweeps you off your feet and carries you off into the moonlight, the One inspired by Hollywood and fairytales. Then there's the one you didn't see coming. The Twin Flame is quite often that unexpected person that shows up in what may feel like the most inopportune time, but in hindsight you find that they were one of the biggest catalysts of your life. Of. Your. Life.

They help you to see who you are. They act as a mirror, a

reflection of the depths of your Self. Sometimes they are even identified by having notable birthmarks or scars that mirror your own. The connection is extremely powerful and intense and the two of you have nearly (sometimes full) telepathic connection. The synchronicities are off the charts, maybe your children carry the same name, your last names were the same, your tattoos, birthdays, hometowns... you feel an uncanny remembrance of them but it doesn't quite make sense. Your soul remembers them. Your heart undergoes an extreme activation.

This heart activation is a signifier of the twin flame union. An uncomfortable feeling of a literal explosion within the heart chakra followed by memories or visions of past lives with one another. Please note though that this union must not need to go on once the activation has occurred. You will feel a certain magic unfolding all around you in all layers of your life and you will desire to hold on to this relationship that has ignited your inner fire. The 'flame' has been lit. Twin flame relationships are commonly marked by a pattern of one partner buckling under the intensity and 'running', thus beginning the characteristic runner-chaser dynamic that can last years, even decades in some twin flame relationships.

At the beginning, the twin flame partner will catalyze and catapult you forward in your spiritual awakening process, teaching you new ideas about love and spirituality, mirroring and stirring up whatever residue of your past needs healing, and challenging your beliefs.

Twin flame journeys are far from comfortable... Marked by extreme joy and fiery passion, deep loving connection and all of the extreme opposites: extreme pain and heartache, painful separation. If you search 'twin flame journey' in YouTube or google or on Instagram you will find countless stories of twin flames and their struggles to find union. You will find just as many stories of twin flame counterparts who finally decided to give up the fight after much pain and anguish. You will find far fewer stories of happy reunion. Because these relationships take a great deal of work.

Those who make the decision to continue to pursue relationship with twin flame partners often find themselves in years long struggles between separation and 'reunion' with all of the highs and lows of the two on a constant loop. Those that succeed in finding a balanced union report deep profound love.

archetypical relationships

"By three methods we may learn wisdom: First, by reflection, which is the noblest; Second, by imitation, which is the easiest; and Third, by experience, which is the bitterest."

CONFUCIOUS

UNDERSTANDING archetypes in mythology, psychology and spirituality provides a lens for us to understand ourselves and the many relationships in our lives. Many philosophical teachers of the past like Plato, Carl Jung, Joseph Campbell; And David Ngan, Caroline Myss and Ainsley Macleod of present, use the concept of archetypal relationships and soul contracts.

In his book, *The Archetypes and The Collective Unconscious,* Carl Jung broke down 12 key archetypes and in an examination of the 12 Common Archetypes, writer Carl Golden adds clear characteristics of each:

(see next page)

1 the innocent

Motto: free to be you and me
Goal: to be happy
Strategy: to do things right
Greatest Fear: to be punished for doing something bad or wrong
Weakness: boring for all their naive innocence
Talent: faith and optimism
Also Known As: *utopian, traditionalist, naive, mystic, saint, romantic, dreamer*

2 the orphan

Motto: all men and women are created equal
Goal: to belong
Strategy: develop ordinary solid virtues, be down to earth, the common touch
Greatest Fear: to be left out or to stand out from the crowd
Weakness: losing one's own self in an effort to blend in or for the sake of superficial relationships
Talent: realism, empathy
Also Known As: *the good old boy, the person next door, the realist, the solid citizen, the good neighbor, the silent majority*

3 the hero

Motto: where there's a will, there's a way
Goal: expert mastery in a way that improves the world
Strategy: to be as strong and competent as possible
Greatest Fear: weakness, vulnerability, being a "chicken"
Weakness: arrogance, always needing another battle to fight
Talent: competence and courage
Also Known As: *the warrior, crusader, rescuer, superhero, the soldier, the winner*

4 the mother/ caregiver

Motto: love your neighbour as yourself
Goal: to help others
Strategy: doing things for others
Greatest Fear: selfishness and ingratitude
Weakness: martyrdom and being exploited
Talent: compassion, generosity
Also Known As: *the saint, altruist, parent, helper, supporter*

5 the explorer

Motto: don't fence me in
Goal: to experience a better, more authentic, more fulfilling life
Strategy: journey, seeking out and experiencing new things, escape from boredom
Greatest Fear: getting trapped, conformity, and inner emptiness
Weakness: aimless wandering, becoming a misfit
Talent: autonomy, ambition, being true to one's soul
Also Known As: *the seeker, iconoclast, wanderer, individualist, pilgrim*

6 the rebel

Motto: rules are made to be broken
Goal: to overturn what isn't working
Strategy: disrupt, destroy, or shock
Greatest Fear: to be powerless
Weakness: crossing over to the dark side, crime
Talent: outrageousness, radical freedom
Also Known As: *the rebel, revolutionary, wild man or woman, the misfit, or iconoclast*

7 the lover

Motto: you're the only one
Goal: being in a relationship with the people, work and surroundings they love
Strategy: to become more and more physically and emotionally attractive
Greatest Fear: being alone, a wallflower, unwanted, unloved
Weakness: outward-directed desire to please others at risk of losing own identity
Talent: passion, gratitude, appreciation, and commitment
Also Known As: *the partner, friend, intimate, enthusiast, sensualist, spouse, team-builder*

8 the creator

Motto: if you can imagine it, it can be done
Goal: to realize a vision
Strategy: develop artistic control and skill
Greatest Fear: mediocre vision or execution
Weakness: perfectionism, bad solutions
Talent: creativity and imagination
Also Known As: *the artist, inventor, innovator, musician, writer or dreamer*

9 the jester

Motto: you only live once
Goal: to have a great time and lighten up the world
Strategy: play, make jokes, be funny
Greatest Fear: being bored or boring others
Weakness: frivolity, wasting time
Talent: joy
Also Known As: *the fool, trickster, joker, practical joker or comedian*

---

10 the sage

Motto: the truth will set you free
Goal: to use intelligence and analysis to understand the world
Strategy: seeking out information and knowledge; self-reflection and understanding thought processes
Greatest Fear: being duped, misled—or ignorance
Weakness: can study details forever and never act
Talent: wisdom, intelligence
Also Known As: *the expert, scholar, detective, advisor, thinker, philosopher, thinker, teacher*

---

11 the magician

Motto: I make things happen
Goal: to make dreams come true
Strategy: develop a vision and live by it
Greatest Fear: unintended negative consequences
Weakness: becoming manipulative
Talent: finding win-win solutions
Also Known As: *the visionary, catalyst, inventor, charismatic leader, shaman, healer, medicine man*

---

12 the ruler

Motto: power isn't everything, it's the only thing
Goal: create a prosperous, successful family or community
Strategy: exercise power
Greatest Fear: chaos, being overthrown
Weakness: being authoritarian, unable to delegate
Talent: responsibility, leadership
Also Known As: *the boss, leader, aristocrat, king, queen, politician*

Reviewing your Self and others through the lens of archetypes can help you to gain acceptance and compassion. Determining which archetype(s) align with an individual helps us to understand and accept dispositions, personalities, strengths, weaknesses, attachments, and values. We are who we are. Recognizing archetypal roles within our relationships can help us see that many of the patterns and dynamics of our relationships are Universal and more common than we know, and thus can help us to gain acceptance.

2.01 Exercise

INTENTION: Examine the relationship archetypes in your life

ACTION: Determine your own archetype(s) *(you may be a combination of more than one)* and think about five or more key relationships in your life. In your journal or on a loose sheet of paper create a chart with 3 columns. In the first column write the name of one person, In the second column write the archetype(s) you associate them with. Take some time to sit with the information listed on the previous pages of Jung's characteristics of each archetype and allow yourself time to embrace the characteristics of this person and accept them for who they are. If this person brings up negative feelings for you, take time and space to breathe through those feelings and allow yourself to see their positive traits. In the third column write down their strengths/talents. Do you admire these strengths? Have you inherited some of these talents? What have they taught you about your self?

EFFECT: With understanding and acceptance we can shift the energy of existing relationships and inspire powerful change... Whether that means change within a relationship or moving forward and leaving a relationship.

The Chemistry of Attachment

> Attachment is attachment to conditions
> of return or security or comfort or joy, and
> our work is to find these things within our
> Selves. Our work is to learn to love un-
> conditionally.

ATHENA ALLREAD

IMAGINE yourself as four years old. You've just found a sweet yellow baby bird at the base of a beautiful giant oak tree. This sweet baby bird is chirping and singing. You kneel down to pick it up. You are immediately overcome with the urge to keep this baby bird forever. You love the way it feels in your hands, so soft, you love the sounds of it chirping, so innocent, and you want nothing more than to take care of it. You carry this birdie around all day introducing it to your world. Instinct tells you to return birdie to a big oak tree where you found it but you're not ready to let go of this little birdie. You squeeze it tightly in your little hands not wanting to let go. That little birdie is ready to test out its wings. The time has come for you to let him go.

At the onset of your meeting with little birdie, your young brain experiences a series of very real physiological and chemical responses. The immediate feelings of joy and hyper-focused attention on this little birdie (an increase in dopamine), the desire to care for this little birdie (a release of oxytocin), the desire to keep it forever (a little more of that oxytocin), and your inability to think about anything other than this little birdie (a decrease in serotonin). The chemical response of your entire nervous system has taken over and made it difficult for you to think rationally about the needs of this little birdie. You have become attached.

Your physiological system operates independently of your mind and rational 'thoughts.' When you come into contact with others, a series of chemical reactions occurs within both your energetic system and your physiological system that can feel to be outside of your control. The reactions will vary in severity based on several factors like your childhood experiences and conditioning, past life connection with this person, present state of awareness.

There are little chemical messengers running through our bodies that are carriers of our stories and have much to share if we will listen.

If you desire to build, maintain and experience healthy loving relationships in this life, you will benefit from understanding the role of these messengers and your own brain chemistry in the experience.

Fascinated by the neuroscience of love and connection, I came across the philanthropic brain research organization The DANA Foundation in my research. In their studies of "companionate love" DANA researchers break down the emotion systems in the brain used for mating, reproduction, and the rearing of young into: lust, attraction, and attachment. They correlate each emotion system with a specific neurobiology in the brain.

In humans, attachment is characterized by feelings of calm, security, social comfort, and emotional union. DANA describes attachment in the brain as being *primarily associated with the neuropeptides oxytocin and vasopressin, hypothesizing that the system of 'Attachment' evolved primarily to motivate individuals to sustain their affiliations long enough to complete the parental duties of their species.*

Additional chemical processes of attachment in the brain

manifest with feelings of romantic attraction, associated with increased levels of the neurotransmitters dopamine and norepinephrine and with lower levels of serotonin.

DANA describes these shifts in the brain and their associations. Increased levels of dopamine are associated with heightened attention, motivation, and goal-directed behaviors. *Increased concentrations of dopamine and norepinephrine in the brain have been shown to be associated with excessive energy, euphoria, loss of appetite, increased mental activity, hyperactivity, and decreased need for sleep.* These are all reactions that most of us have experienced or will experience in love. We experience these feelings and reactions with best friends, lovers, close family members, our work, and especially with our children.

Understanding our brain chemistry and its role in attachment can help us to understand the dynamics of unhealthy attachments. On a physiological level, we quite easily move from attraction into infatuation and then into obsession with increased levels of norepinephrine and lowered levels of serotonin. Scientists have discovered that the decreased levels of serotonin found in people who are in the early phases of 'romantic love' are comparable to the lower levels of serotonin found in people diagnosed with obsessive compulsive disorder. If you yourself have ever experienced those irrational feelings of obsession over a romantic love interest, then you can now understand that there is an actual chemical process taking place within your brain and with that understanding you can begin to seize back control and utilize tools like visualization, supplementation, herbs, diet to rebalance those hormones.

Because *you* have the power to control your thoughts, you have the power to alter your own brain chemistry. Scientific studies on individuals in meditation have shown the power of meditation and thought in shifting the actual chemistry of the brain. We have so much power!

With the use of the mind, awareness, observation we can steady our own chemistry and free ourselves from attachment. Once I asked Spirit, "Is there any attachment that's good?" I heard a very clear "No." "Because when we love, we love without attachment. Attachment is attachment to conditions of return or security or comfort or joy, and our work is to find these things within our Selves. Our work is to learn to love unconditionally."

2.02 Exercise

INTENTION: Utilize affirmations as a powerful tool for altering our thinking and our brain chemistry

ACTION: As needed, repeat the following healthy relationship affirmations. Repeat a minimum of three times to ensure impact.

I gratefully receive this relationship for all that it is.

I let go with ease and full acceptance of surrounding circumstances.

I fearlessly accept Your love.

I lovingly release my Self from all attachment in this relationship.

I unconditionally love You.

I gratefully share my Self with you and thank you for sharing your Self with me.

I trust in the power of love.

I accept Your love without condition.

EFFECT: Using these daily affirmations you will begin to shed fear and limiting beliefs and shift into a loving space of gratitude, power and acceptance.

3

METAMORPHOSIS

Metamorphosis

We are all butterflies.
Earth is our chrysalis.
LEEANN TAYLOR

METAMORPHOSIS is the process of transformation from an immature form to a mature adult form, commonly associated with frogs and butterflies. *You* are a butterfly preparing to emerge from your chrysalis. You've completed a cycle of growth, you've stepped into that chrysalis which may in some ways feel like a period of stillness, and in others a very dark period (See Chapter Nine - The Dark Night), and as your period of suffering is ending and you are outgrowing your chrysalis, you are preparing to spread your wings and take off!

How do you know when you are outgrowing your chrysalis and when it is time to take flight? Imagine the chrysalis to be like a shell that you will shed when you are ready, and that shell represents the old self, old relationships, old habits. In order to hold space for the New (new self, new relationships, new opportunities). We are usually guided to begin clearing out the old when the time has come to spread our wings. That guidance may come as minor irritations at your current situation, actual verbal encouragement from others who love and care about you, a soft nudge to begin exploring new job opportunities, a hard kick in the form of a dramatic event... or just a gut feeling that something new is coming in. Before you ever even make the decision to leave a relationship, chances are you've already begun to undergo your own process of metamorphosis.

Your period of metamorphosis could be of mind, body and of spirit. Perhaps you're in recovery and have worked through the beautiful transformative process of 12-Steps, perhaps you've worked with a therapist and outgrown old beliefs of unworthiness, perhaps you've overcome a major physical limitation...

My client Hannah experienced a major transformation of her physical body after losing over one hundred pounds. When she came to me, she was glowingly healthy and positive, receiving unbelievable job offers as she was completing her doctorate studies, she had a strong inner circle of friends, a loving husband, and yet she had subtle feelings of unfulfillment. She didn't understand where these feelings were coming from and knew in her mind that she should be completely happy and at peace, yet she wasn't. In one of her sessions I had her recap her weekend away with her husband. On the surface, it felt like a perfect weekend... Charming Victorian seaside town, delicious restaurants, sweet little bed & breakfast. But as she shared her experience, Spirit pointed out to me a sudden feeling that had come over her while at lunch with her husband. *'The feeling and thought that passed through her mind in that moment is the key to understanding her unfulfillment,'* Spirit said. There, in my mind's eye, I saw that in one very swift moment of sitting with her husband at lunch, the thought passed through her mind: *'Is this it?'*

I asked her if she'd had such a thought. And she admitted that yes, she had. She made light of the exact tone of the *'Is this it?'* and we giggled a bit, but then came the true realization that *'this'* was not what she wanted.

Hannah had outgrown her relationship with her husband. In

her own metamorphosis, they were no longer in alignment. He had much of his own growth to experience still and she had far surpassed him. She was now presented with the difficult choice of whether to stay in that place of unfulfillment, or to move forward and create space for fulfillment. She chose to create space and within no time that space was filled with a very fulfilling relationship that provided her with the new level of depth and connection that she was seeking.

Hannah's process of metamorphosis is what many Spiritualists call Ascension. Ascension is the departur from what you've known, opening your heart to a new experience and choosing consciously expand into the unknown. It is the upward movement of the Spirit through understanding, grace, and awareness into Higher Consciousness. In Hannah's case, she literally shed the physical weight that had manifested as a byproduct of other stressors in her life. Through physical transformation, dedication to her self, therapy, and shamanic healing, she rose to a place of understanding, grace and Higher Consciousness. The great masters of our past like Jesus, Mother Mary, Gautama Buddha, Kwan Yin, ascended as they shed the pain and hurts of their experiences on earth and moved into complete forgiveness, love, and compassion. They arrived at this Higher Consciousness through a process of journey and shedding of indiscriminate attachments, release of ego, their service to humanity, and their work with Spirit.

You are reaching for Higher Consciousness now. If you've picked up this book, then you have already experienced or are already undergoing your process of metamorphosis and ascension. You will soon be able to move into complete forgiveness, love and compassion and spread *your* wings and fly!

No, it's not easy... but you can do it! It is so freeing when we shed the weight of old stress, attachments, resentments and unforgiveness.

When you find yourself ascending, it is very difficult to maintain old relationships with those who are not rising alongside or near you. Trust that we are all evolving and that all those whom you love and care for will grow wings of their own in their own timing, and it is not your responsibility to determine when and how they do so. Honor each person's own natural process.

3.01 Exercise

INTENTION: Marvel at the beauty of your own Metamorphosis

ACTION: Find a place to lie down. Give yourself 5-10 minutes (or more if you like!) to rest and move into visualization. Begin to imagine a beautiful sunny day, sunlight peeking through the branches in a large oak tree. Hanging from one of those branches is a large brown chrysalis and you are now lying inside of it. Imagine yourself with wings... Maybe you're a butterfly, but maybe you're a fairy or an angel or simply just you with wings. Feel into your elbows and back and genuinely imagine what it must feel like to have these wings. Feel yourself in that crouching position, knees up, ready to stretch out of this shell. But first, take a moment to take inventory of your life up to this point. Where were you before here? How have you grown? What have you already shed? Take this moment to celebrate how far you've come. Now imagine using your elbows and feet to begin to press through the limits of this cocoon. Feel your legs being freed, your head and arms being freed. Feel into the fear and flutters of excitement in the heart at this new point of departure. You are ready to take flight. What will you do? How far will you go? Who will you become? Take some time to journal your thoughts and feelings after completing this visualization.

EFFECT: After completing this visualization, you will recognize just how far you've come, and just how natural it is to have those feelings of fear and heart flutters as you prepare for take-off.

4

KARMA & RELATIONSHIP ROLES

KARMA & RELATIONSHIP ROLES

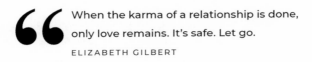 When the karma of a relationship is done,
only love remains. It's safe. Let go.
ELIZABETH GILBERT

KARMA is a belief in the flow of energy from one source to another. As it flows between sources, there is a constant striving attempt to be in balance. A balancing between polarities. Those sources can be two people, a person and an entity or cause, or two aspects of one person, the energy flows through intentions, actions, service, and deeds.

Traditionally a concept based in Hinduism and Buddhism, karma is now common course in western culture, language and philosophy. Encyclopædia Britannica defines Karma as a spiritual principle of cause and effect where intent and actions of an individual (cause) influence the future of that individual (effect).

Some believe that good intent and good deeds contribute to good karma and thus future happiness, while bad intent and bad deeds contribute to bad karma and future suffering. The karmic cycle continues over the course of a lifetime and in and out of many lifetimes. Your soul has endless opportunities to balance out its own karma.

Our interpersonal relationships are some of our greatest means for balancing karma. As a shaman (and a human!) I do believe that how we walk on earth is a great factor in our karma, such as how we treat the plants, animals, the earth itself, but I also believe that how we treat others and allow for them to treat us, how we give and how we receive and how we *take*, this is our gateway for achieving the greatest balance in our karma.

givers

"For it is in giving that we receive."
ST. FRANCIS OF ASSISI

I'd like to emphasize the 'allowing others' piece. My mother was a woman who was in service of others all her life. She was a mother to all, opening up her home to those who needed shelter, cooking, delivering and providing food for those in need, caring for the children of young mothers, donating her meager earnings wherever she saw a dire need, a dedicated member of service at her church. Yet she never allowed anyone to 'give' back to her. In the end of her life, she found herself physically disabled and requiring the complete care of others. At the end of her life, I believe her greatest karmic lesson was to learn to 'receive' and allow others to take care of *her*.

This is the archetype of the Great Mother. She fears selfishness and ingratitude and subjects herself to martyrdom and unnecessary suffering. One of her great challenges and karmic lessons is learning to allow *herself* to be cared for. Male or female you may find yourself under the archetype of the Great Mother. If so, are you allowing others to help you?

The Great Mother can support others in fulfilling their karmic duties to 'give' by allowing them to help her meet her needs. There is an immense joy and satisfaction and sense of fulfillment that we experience when giving. Why not share in that satisfaction? Trust that when you receive, you are giving someone else the joy and satisfaction that comes with *giving*.

takers

"Allow others to give you loving care. Receive
without guilt or apologies."
ST. FRANCIS OF ASSISI

What about 'takers'? Are we '*allowing*' them to take? Well... possibly yes... On a soul level, you may have agreed with the soul of another to take on certain archetypal roles so that you might each learn valuable soul lessons. Think of it as a great stage play where you've elected certain roles for the experience. The dynamic between giver and taker, for example, can bring together the archetypal Great Mother/Lover and the Rebel/Ruler. This pairing often leads to abusive relationship dynamics. Where the loyal committed Mother/Lover allows the Rebel/Ruler to take control. A balance within this dynamic can be found when the Mother/Lover is able to stand up and release her (or his) fears of being alone and beliefs surrounding unworthiness and 'selfishness'; and when the Rebel/Ruler is able to release his (or her) fears around loss of power and authority. Finding that healthy karmic balance within the abusive relationship dynamic can certainly be found through counseling, therapy, self-work and concerted effort; But many times, through the process of metamorphosis, the Mother/Lover grows her wings of confidence long before the Rebel/Ruler is willing to shed their shell of authoritarianism and leaves the relationship.

My client Christina came to me for a soul retrieval. In her 44 years she'd overcome abandonment, childhood abuse, alcohol abuse, domestic abuse and was ready to recover the beautiful parts of her Self which had been taken away from her in those experiences. In the soul retrieval we were guided by Spirit back to very specific events in her life. We gathered up her youthful cheery self at age 17, we gathered up her feisty self from the first moment she stood up to her abusive husband, and several other versions of her Self that were ready to return and support her. Later she shared with me stories of her childhood and being born to a young mother who was also in an abusive relationship which ended when she was just 6 months old. She shared with me the loving experiences within the home of her grandparents before she was returned to her mother and underwent several years of physical and sexual abuse of her father. When she was of age she quickly married and found herself under the care of a husband who at first fulfilled her needs for safety and security. Christina explained to me how her husband first kindly offered to take control of the finances to save her the stress of being involved. He promised to take care of her. But over the period of ten years his desire for control escalated to him demanding that she not open the mail, him controlling her bank cards, turning them on and off, having a secret combination lock suitcase that he kept beside the bed, and eventually physical abuse, stalking and manipulation.

Through the realization of her need to allow others to help her Christina began to gently navigate the exit of that relationship. This realization came through witnessing the suffering of her children and finally in the form of her loving grandparents saying to her that no matter what he took away, they would help her. Through family support, domestic violence support organizations, therapy, shamanic healing and self-study, Christina freed herself from that relationship, gained an understanding of the relationship dynamic, found acceptance, and now lives a free and happy life with her son in a beautiful home of her own.

If you are reading this book and seeking to navigate your way out of an abusive relationship (mentally, emotionally or physically abusive), allow others to help you out. Reach out for support, find healing for the parts of your Self that have been taken through journaling, counseling and support groups. You have already begun your process of metamorphosis and sooner than you know, you will be spreading your wings and taking flight.

Remember that in allowing others to give to you, you are allowing for them to experience the joy, satisfaction and fulfillment of giving and you are also allowing for a natural balancing of karma to occur.

4.01 Exercise

INTENTION: Karmic review of a key past and/or present relationship

ACTION: Consider journaling the following. Think of a relationship dynamic that was/is particularly uncomfortable for you. Think back to the section on archetypes and roles... What do you know now of the dynamic between yourself and the other party? What have they taught you about yourself and the world? What did you teach them? What did they give you? What have you given them? Take a moment to meditate and tune in to where there may have been or may still be opportunity of recognition, balancing and release of a karmic pattern.

EFFECT: Understanding your relationship karma and the patterns of flow of energy from your Self to another helps you to more easily spot imbalances as they arise and to take action in getting into a healthy flow. That action could fall anywhere between leaving a relationship with an unhealthy flow to attempting to restore balance to that flow.

Relationships as Teachers

 Even upon metamorphosis of the new Self, there is still the opportunity to be a valuable teacher for one another.

ATHENA ALLREAD

What if we viewed each relationship as a teacher along our path of learning? Once we've learned some key lessons (balanced out some karma), we graduate on and move into new learning experiences with new teachers. What if you could consciously choose when you'd like to begin working with a new teacher? You can! You have full free will to choose how and when you enter into new relationships. In romantic relationships, some individuals begin their relationships in adolescence and choose to stay with that partner/teacher for the remainder of their life. This is beautiful. Some individuals begin their romantic relationships later in life after having already learned a great deal about themselves. And some individuals choose to experience several meaningful relationships over the course of adulthood. Although our culture places high value on longevity in relationships, all of these varied paths of relationship present dynamic opportunities to learn about your Self and your partner/teachers.

Yet, why do we confront such judgement when we choose to

leave relationships and move on to new teachers? If you're reading this, it's likely that you have confronted judgement from within or judgement from the outside world. Many people experience a great sense of guilt and sometimes shame for choosing to leave a relationship path they've been on. Because of our conditioning we may have been led to believe that our only choice is to remain with one teacher for the duration of our lives. This commonly manifests as parents or trusted advisors encouraging you to stay in an unfulfilling marriage or job when you know deep within your Self that you are ready for new learning experiences and greater fulfillment. Understanding that perhaps they've chosen that path but that you have free will to choose your own path, you can begin to free yourself from the energies of judgement.

If you're choosing to leave a relationship with one teacher in order to fulfill your inner need for growth, expansion and new learning experiences, know that when you make this choice, especially if that choice is made with love, the Universe loves and supports you tenfold. Trust that this Universe is kind and compassionate and loves you no matter what. You are here to love and you are here to learn! Take risks, follow the guidance of your heart, and don't let judgement stop you from making your great offering to your Self and humanity.

With many of my clients, friends, inner circles, I see both men and women who find themselves far along their spiritual path, and find that when their partner is not walking alongside them, they begin to feel and experience a sense of disconnect. Imagine yourself hiking up a mountainside along the Appalachian trail with a partner, stopping to see the sights, turning to share in the wonder and realizing that your partner is far back along the trail. In these moments of disconnect, there is an ascension into a new level of consciousness of one partner. As that disconnect widens it can become more and more difficult to share in the wonder...

to engage and connect on a conscious 'soul' level. The conscious partner is in a moment of wonder while the other partner might be remaining still under that illusion of comfort (See Chapter 1 section - Illusion of Comfort). There is no wrong in resting in the stillness; however under that state of rest the discomfort will be felt as the ascending partner drifts higher and higher and further and further away. When you become more conscious, everything changes: your diets and drinking preferences will change, circle of friends will change, habits and choice of leisure activities may change. This is all a part of your metamorphosis. The person you once were will gradually dissolve as the new "Higher" self emerges. Even upon metamorphosis of the new Self, there is still the opportunity to be a valuable teacher for one another. Like a crossing on that Appalachian Trail... This is the check-in point for many relationships when they must decide how they will proceed forward.

4.02 Exercise

INTENTION: Teachers, Wonders and Gratitude Inventory

ACTION: Imagine the relationship under review as a journey along the Appalachian trail. You've been hiking along with this person (group or organization) and you've taken in some really beautiful sights along the way. Take an inventory of the wonders of this journey together thus far. What were some of the beautiful moments you've shared? What were some of your more positive experiences? What gifts did they give you? What qualities did you develop along your journey together? What have you learned from one another? Write it all down in a safe place where you can come back to whenever you are having difficulty moving forward.

EFFECT: Recognizing the wonder and gifts of time spent along a journey together with another can shift us away from those paralyzing questions of 'why' when we're stuck in the past. We can look at the past with love and light and turn back to the beautiful journey that we're on and continue upward. There are many more wonders to be experienced if you are willing to continue moving forward.

5

THE SEVEN DEMONS
OF CHANGE

Stepping onto the Battlefield of Change

Growth is painful. Change is painful.
But nothing is as painful as staying
stuck somewhere you don't belong.

N.R. NARAYANA MURTHY

We change.

Intentions change.

When do we decide that it's time to *make* a change? What inspires us to reassess and re-define our values? What is it that propels us forward? Commonly, it's some form of suffering: financial suffering, emotional suffering, or physical suffering... a catalytic circumstance or event... and can come in varying degrees of intensity from mild to unbearable. Some people make a change after experiencing mild discomfort and some need extreme pain and/or trauma to be moved forward... It all depends on your unique threshold for pain. There is no definitive explanation for why one person is more resilient than another or why one person has a higher threshold for pain than another although some theorists speculate that thresholds increase with sustained pain over time. Ultimately, it's your choice how long and to what degree you will stand for the pain. Think of what pains you as you would think of a headache. You can choose to sit with a headache for hours or you can choose to take action... Drink water, take an Advil, get some rest... Free yourself from the pain. Otherwise it may cripple you.

We decide to make a change when we are ready to move in the direction of our own wellbeing, happiness and freedom. We come to a point where we recognize that our own wellbeing, happiness and freedom is an important contributor to the overall wellbeing of our inner and outer circles, our families, our workplaces, the greater collective, our planet.

When arriving to the decision to leave relationships in pursuit of happiness and freedom, we are at the gateway of a great battlefield of transition. At the other end of this battlefield is greater wellbeing, happiness, pleasure, freedom, enlightenment, the potential for the greatest loves you've ever known... but in pursuit you will come across many obstacles and what I call the Seven Demons of Relationship Transition. These demons are the emotional blocks that will arise as you make your way across the battlefield. They will attempt to block and stop you and I will provide you with tools for slaying them one by one as they come, and trusting in your Self and your own strength and power as you continue forward.

the seven demons of relationship transition

It's often easier to confront an external enemy than to confront one's inner demons.

RAM DASS

Entering into a period of relationship transition can be like stepping onto a battlefield filled with demons, there to block us, battle us and hold us hostage as we make our best attempts to get to the other side. Our souls know that at the other side lies our happiness and freedom and once we've gathered enough courage, we suit up, pull ourselves and our resources together and step out onto that field.

It is important that you know that no matter which role you play as you step onto the battlefield of transition, whether you are the initiator or the opposing force, you will come across many, if not all, of these demons.

There are seven key demons that we face on the battlefield. These 'demons' show up as psychological defense and coping mechanisms and energies that act in opposition of love. They dim our lights, hold us hostage in the darkness, and limit us from moving forward and thriving. In a relationship transition, these demons are natural energies that we'll encounter on our journey across that battlefield, however we MUST slay them each time we come into contact with them or they will come back again and again.

For each demon, I'll share tools and exercises for looking at them head on, slaying them, and leaving them behind.

The Seven (7) Demons of Relationship Transition:

1. Ambivalence
2. Denial
3. Fear
4. Guilt
5. Anger
6. Shame
7. Hurt

the demon of ambivalence

"In these times I don't, in a manner of speaking, know what I want; perhaps I don't want what I know and want what I don't know."
MARSILIO FICINO, *THE LETTERS OF MARSILIO FICINO, VOL. 3*

NOT so ironically... As I wrote this book this section was where I took a 3 month break. Initially I stepped away to endure a cold miserable winter, but also... I hit a writer's block around the concept of ambivalence. In seeking to understand ambivalence to a degree at which I could intelligibly write about it... Spirit actually placed me into an 'ambivalent' cocoon of sorts. What I came out with is this: During our periods of ambivalence, nothing happens. We don't take action. We sit on things. We sit on our plans, our dreams, our existing relationships and we limit ourselves from moving forward into anything greater. Yes, I do believe in magnetism and at times as we sit, the Universe is slowly bringing in closer that which we desire. Sometimes a period of rest is just what's needed for us to experience in greater context the things that will thrust us forward. I learned to question and be clear when I slow down, 'Am I under a period of rest? Or am I under a period of ambivalence?' And how do we differentiate between the two? A period of rest is a well-deserved break after a period of hard work and exertion. Ambivalence is a stand-still.

In the Personality and Social Psychology Bulletin on Attitudinal Ambivalence, ambivalence is defined as the mental disharmony or disconnect a person feels when having both positive and negative feelings regarding the same individual. Psychologically uncomfortable ambivalence, also known as cognitive dissonance, can lead to unsupportive behaviors like avoidance and procrastination.

Ambivalence is the first Demon that many of us meet when stepping out onto the battlefield. Imagine Jabba the Hut from Star Wars... This demon sluggishly stands in our way, each move we make it shifts its weight directly in front of us. And we do a dance of sorts back and forth attempting to dodge and sway out of its way. Slow dancing back and forth in battle with this demon we become jaded and consider giving up before we've even taken any big strides onto the battlefield. *Perhaps it's not worth the struggle,* we think. You're at a standstill, feeling split and/or unmotivated to move in any direction. Either way you move, you feel that Jabba the Hutt will be there blocking you. You feel like no matter what, you can't win. On this battlefield, the Demon of Ambivalence appears so large that we feel exhausted even attempting to 'think' of ways around it. Facing this enormous demon, we accept a momentary defeat as we sway back and forth in our minds between giving up completely (avoidance) or maybe coming back to try again later (procrastination).

You *must* move further out onto the battlefield if you desire to find true happiness and freedom. You *must* take those first fearful steps to find your way forward. In most cases, there comes a time when a decision has to be made or it is made for you. My dear friend Jennifer* was in her own state of ambivalence in her fading marriage. She'd made her best efforts at reconnection but felt no sense of urgency to end it and thus was not initiating a separation with her husband. That is until he surprised her with the news that he wanted a divorce and was going to be leaving their home and moving in with his new girlfriend. A decision had been made. This is a very common story I've heard time and time again. One partner feels they have 'time' and takes no action, and is surprised by a seemingly sudden decision being made by the other. And soon follows a traumatic whirlwind of change and upheaval. If you find yourself in this situation, be gentle with yourself. It doesn't matter whether you saw it coming or not, what matters is that forward movement is happening.

We experience the greatest discomfort from our ambivalence at the times when a decision has to be made or is made *for us*.

The ego takes a hit when the reigns of control that we thought we held are seized by another party. We cannot control or prevent others from making their own free will choices, but what we can do is make choices for our Selves and control our personal responses to the choices others make. It is very difficult to accept the choices that others make when they have a direct negative impact on us in the moment, but acceptance is the fastest way to find peace.

Following acceptance, trust will be your guide to shift you into a lighter version of your Self. See the affirmations at the end of this section for help with acceptance and trust.

The Demon of Ambivalence steps in at the entryway to the battlefield of transition. He meets us there when decisions need to be made. He holds us hostage, creates a wall, a barrier, a block that prohibits us from moving forward. *This* is our first obstacle on our way to the other side.

INTENTION: In the face of the Demon of Ambivalence we often freeze in place. Are you in a standstill with yourself? Work, love, whatever it is... If you are feeling stuck or frozen try using these affirmations to lift you up and propel you forward.

ACTION: As needed, repeat the following action orienting affirmations. Repeat a minimum of three times to ensure impact.

> *I accept that I cannot control that which I cannot control.*
> *I release fear and I hold trust in the Divine unfoldment of this plan.*
> *I make choices that benefit me.*
> *I trust that what benefits me benefits the greater good.*
> *I allow myself to make mistakes, pick back up, and keep going.*
> *I see that with each mistake I've made, I've taken a step further forward.*
> *I take the steps I am guided to take, one step at a time, one day at a time.*

EFFECT: Repeating these affirmations will support you in accepting what is and moving forward one step at a time.

the demon of denial

"Pain can be endured and defeated only if it is embraced.
Denied or feared, it grows."

DEAN KOONTZ

THE Demon of Denial, like a raven in the night, swoops down from the sky, directly over our heads dropping a dark cloak over our eyes, crippling and prohibiting us from seeing clearly. Depending on the density of the fabric of that cloak, we end up with either a very limited view or none at all.. Unlike the Demon of Ambivalence standing larger than life in front of us, in the face of this demon our vision itself is obscured. We are no longer simply frozen in place... now we are blind.

The Demon of Denial takes away our sight, prohibiting us from seeing behind us, beside us, and in front of us. It holds us hostage from truth and from freedom. Suddenly the stories of our past, present and sometimes future experiences are altered to better suit our resistance to moving forward. We convince ourselves that painful events that happened didn't in fact happen in the ways we remember, we justify inexcusable actions and behaviors. We quiet that tiny voice inside begging us to see *the truth* that it's time to let go and move forward. We fear letting go and so we hang on. We change our stories just a bit so that we can hang on just a bit longer.

Both men and women come under the veil of the Demon of Denial as they take their early steps onto the battlefield of transition.

Nicholas* came to me as he neared the end of a decade long love relationship. He recognized that their time in partnership had come to an end, and yet he struggled with letting go. In our session his guides urged him to release the energetic cords tying him not only to her, but to others in his periphery whose judgements were clouding his 'view' and interfering with him clearly seeing his way forward. When I connected in with his partners' energy and impact on him, I saw large razor sharp claws in his shoulder. Not surprisingly he had experienced physical pain in that very shoulder. Shoulder pain is quite common in those battling with the Demon of Denial.

Those large razor sharp claws represented domination and control. After so many years of codependency, Nicholas was not ready to free himself from that piercing grip his partner. For months he struggled with his own visions of their past, present and future. The Demon of Denial laid veil over the manipulation, judgement, harsh mistreatment he'd faced in his years with her, and he was left to fear losing the woman he only saw to be intelligent, beautiful and charming. Not only does this demon shield the ugly, but it convinces us that we are not worthy of better. It convinces us that we cannot do better. Nicholas grappled with fear and disbelief over whether any woman would be as intelligent and charming as his ex-partner.

How do you differentiate on the battlefield, whether you are facing the Demon of Denial or whether you can and should simply accept your partners' actions and behaviors as character flaws?

The answer I hear from Spirit is to ask yourself...

Have I been mistreated?

If your answer is yes, then you still have a choice. It is not a matter of choosing to accept a behavior, it's a matter of choosing to accept mistreatment. You have complete free will in this human experience to accept whatever you choose.

Do you choose to accept mistreatment?

If your answer is yes, then I don't know that I can help you across that battlefield to freedom. Abuse is defined as mistreatment, cruelty, violence against a person or animal. If you choose to allow another person or entity to abuse you, you will likely find yourself in a repeating cycle, an ongoing battle with the Demon of Denial. But it is never too late to step out. Death itself is not the end. These cycles will repeat lifetime and lifetime again. It will always be your choice whether to remain in that cycle or to end it.

If you answer no, and choose to reject mistreatment, read on for how you can slay that Demon of Denial.

Denial is acting as if a painful event, thought or feeling did not occur. It allows us to momentarily be as present as we can so that we can be with our current realities. Women in domestic abuse situations sometimes utilize denial so that they can coast through for the sake of their children. Women who depend financially on their partner sometimes utilize denial for what they believe to be their only source for survival. Both groups of women are also under a state of paralysis, also facing that Demon of Ambivalence (amongst others). If you are currently in a relationship where you have been or are currently being mistreated, please be gentle with yourself. Ease your way forward. Gradually remove the veil and gently allow yourself to see the truth of your past, present and future. Is denial easier than facing the truth? No. The truth is that ahead of you and all around you lies unconditional love and liberation, and there is nothing easier to face than love.

But to get there, we must first slay that demon of denial.

Most likely if you've been under the veil of the Demon of Denial, you've at some point in your life developed a severe sense of unworthiness. We slay this Demon with fierce confidence and a strong awareness of our own Power and a willingness to remove the veil that has blinded us.

5.02 Exercise

INTENTION: Remove the veil that is blinding you.

ACTION: Pause. Imagine a heavy blanket or veil is covering your face and body. Underneath, you cannot see anything around you. Light comes through but everything is distorted. What could be outside of the cover that you are afraid to look at? Journal and write down the visions and outcomes that you fear. What present and future scenario would you *want* to see if you removed the veil? What are you not seeing that you need to see? Sit down for a quiet meditation. Imagine that you can now see one or more options for moving forward laid out in front of you.

EFFECT: Let's celebrate awareness that the outcomes you've feared are not the only possible outcomes! Now that you can see other scenarios and pathways forward, take ahold of the reigns and begin to plan a course of action for moving forward.

the demon of guilt

"There were things I wanted to tell him. But I knew they would hurt
him. So I buried them, and let them hurt me."
JONATHAN SAFRAN FOER

SOMETIMES in life, we come to a crossroads where we make decisions that will hurt, disappoint and/or offend persons of value in our lives. Following those decisions, the Demon of Guilt creeps in. Alongside the Demon of Guilt, often comes emotions of regret and remorse, a much deeper sense of regret... Whereas regret is the sadness that ensues after the decision is made, an action taken or in some cases an inaction, and guilt is the weight felt in having made the decision.

The Demon of Guilt is a heavy weighted gluttonous beast that will pin you down and chomp away at your heart, pushing you further and further away from your heart-centered intentions. Feelings you've felt, decisions you've been nudged from within to make, are all put to question and eaten away by this ravenous Demon. It pins you down on that battlefield placing such oppressive weight and force against your heart that you begin to lose your ability to breathe.

This demon holds us hostage and forces us to watch repeated loops of the projections of a story of regret. This could be the story of our parents, our children, our ancestors, our beloved partners and sometimes our own. We sit silently and watch the reel of regret, inheriting the emotions and absorbing the story into our psyche while that Demon of Guilt presses his weight further and further into our hearts. Crushing our spirits.

This crushing sensation shows up as felt weight on the heart, heaviness, sadness, anxiousness, difficulty sleeping.

Guilt itself is an emotional response that occurs when a person believes, accurately or not, that they have committed offense or violated a perceived or learned moral standard. Over the course of our lifetimes and the lifetimes of our families, we have been told what is right and what is wrong and inherited those beliefs as our own. When we take action that is not in alignment with what we've been convinced is 'right,' in comes guilt. Questions of loyalty and moral obligation come in strong with the Demon of Guilt.

We carry guilt in leaving many varied relationship types. Colleague, father, lover, friend. One very common reason I hear from clients at the crossroads of relationship transition, is that they don't want to hurt the other person.

Here's my own story of wanting to go in a different direction with opening my own wellness studio.

Not long after I began my work as a full-time practicing Shaman, I was invited onto a team within a reputable holistic wellness practice in my town, with a team of incredibly gifted practitioners. I was nurtured and given a safe space to practice and grow myself as a shaman and my client base. I enjoyed my time with this team and a time came when we as a whole were under a period of transition with our facility. At the same time that we were undergoing transition as a whole, I was presented with the opportunity to partner with two fellow practitioners and open a wellness studio of our own. As I deliberated over which way to go, I carried great guilt over desiring to support the team that had supported and nurtured my growth as a Shaman. I felt that I had violated my team's vision of moving forward as a whole.

Another example of the Demon of Guilt rising up, is the story of my client Carli who wanted to relocate to a new city and start a new life. She faced the disappointment of her father not wanting her to go, leaving her heavily guilt ridden. She carried guilt over leaving him behind but upon further contemplation realized that she was only seeing him about once every month or two anyway and that it wouldn't change much based on her new geographical location. And so Carli gathered her courage, sold her house at the beach, and moved to the mountains of North Carolina, several hundred miles from home. She felt free, she was happy, and her life and health took an incredibly positive turn following her move.

Why do people make others feel guilty? Fear! Fear of loss. Fear of failure. Fear of having to see their own faults. Fear of autonomy. There are many fears that show up in the face of change.

The above story of myself and of Carli are stories of two women moving along on their journeys and choosing to follow the heart down a new road into a new direction. It takes courage, bravery and trust to move in a new direction down an unknown path. Don't allow those Demons of Fear and Guilt to hold you back.

What if guilt is not felt?

You may or may not feel guilt for your choices, actions or inactions and have someone on the outside telling you that you have committed a wrongdoing. Maybe your partner has committed the wrongdoing and all you want is for them to acknowledge their wrongdoing, to feel remorse… Guilt. Your partner may or may not feel guilt for their actions or inaction, but as we move forward in Love, our biggest work is gaining acceptance no matter the circumstance. This means accepting when you OR your partner have committed what you believe to be a wrongdoing.

How can we accept wrongdoing?

The fastest route to acceptance… is forgiveness.

5.03 Exercise

INTENTION: Slay the Demon of Guilt

ACTION: In your journal or on a blank piece of paper, list the reasons why you feel guilt. Look at your perceptions of wrongdoing, where you feel you've done wrong. Ask yourself 'why did I make the choice I made?'. Have empathy for yourself in the very moment you committed what you believed to be a wrongdoing. Hold an image in your mind of your Self during that time. No matter if it was yesterday, 5 months ago or 5 years ago, visualize your Self as you were. Imagine standing face to face. If it was a wrongdoing that was committed over a period of time, take a moment to analyze that full period of time as one experience. What did you need during that period of time? What were you seeking? What was your intention when you committed the wrongdoing?

Now imagine still standing face to face with your previous Self, placing your right hand on their left shoulder, as if reaching through a mirror, and looking into those hurting eyes. Say to yourself, 'I forgive you. I understand what you needed. I understand what you were seeking. I understand why you had those intentions. And I forgive you.'

EFFECT: Seeing the hurt in your own eyes, accepting and forgiving yourself, frees you from the oppressive grip and weight of that Demon of Guilt.

the demon of shame

"Soul, if you want to learn secrets, your heart must forget about shame and dignity. You are God's lover, yet you worry what people are saying."
RUMI, *THE ESSENTIAL RUMI*

ALTHOUGH similar in vibration to Guilt, Spirit has shared with me some key distinctions between the two. Each is an emotional response to the belief that we've done harm. With Guilt we inherit and carry the weight of these beliefs, we believe we are responsible... With Shame we hide. Guilt being the resulting feelings of empathy and remorse to believing that you have committed offense on others... Shame being the resulting feelings of humiliation and distress on the Self after believing that you have committed offense.

The Demon of Shame is like a flying stingray, hovering over your head casting a dark shadow of worry, carrying the threat of a quick and sharp sting that can activate feelings of humiliation. The Demon of Shame injects you with the poisonous false belief that 'I' am wrong,' when the truth is that it was an 'action' that was *perceived* as wrong. As the Demon of Shame hovers over our heads, we cower and shrink, almost inverting into a childlike position. We hide within ourselves and we feel alone.

Whenever you are feeling shame, look to the inner child within yourself. Ask him/her why they did what they did. A child often times hides an action or mistake made out of belief that it will be perceived or declared wrong by an authority figure. In your situation of wrongdoing, you are the 'child' and the Demon of Shame is the perceived authority figure hovering over your head. My four-year-old daughter will sneak a piece of gum and run and hide because she believes that I will perceive her taking the gum as wrong. I have taught her to ask for permission, and yet at times she cannot resist the urge to take the gum without permission. In adult life, with situations involving infidelity, there was an urge that could not be resisted and the infidel believes that their partner will perceive their actions as wrong. They become filled with shame and may try to 'hide' the interaction. We will go into adultery and infidelity in Chapter 7, but there are many layers involved in the perceptions of right vs. wrong and the potential distress caused as a result. In these situations, I urge both sides of the line to examine what the motivation was for committing the wrongdoing... and begin to compassionately explore how and where the irresistible 'urge' stemmed from. This can be very deeply healing work for both of you.

5.04 Exercise

INTENTION: Slay the Demon of Shame

ACTION: Think of three (3) things in your life that you feel 'ashamed' of. List them. And for each action (or inaction) write the following:

I am ashamed that I _____

I did this because _____

I am not wrong, but my action was _____

I forgive myself for _____

EFFECT: Accept your own conditions of 'right' and 'wrong' and allow others to define that for themselves. Consciously decide whose measures of 'right' and 'wrong' you would like to be held against. Know that you are a beautiful loving extension of all that is, and 'you' have never been 'wrong.'

the demon of anger

"Bitterness is like cancer. It eats upon the host.
But anger is like fire. It burns it all clean."
MAYA ANGELOU

THE Demon of Anger is fast and stocky carnivorous beast, runs in from the sidelines and tackles us down abruptly before we've had a chance to see it coming. This demon forces us to respond to actions against us or those we love that were unfair, unjust, painful, or 'wrong'. This demon can fill us with a strong feeling of wanting to speak up, wanting to act out, wanting to seek justice for a perceived injustice, hurt or threat. As the Demon of Anger tramples us, our bodies respond physically to this attack with increased heart rate, elevated blood pressure, and increased levels of adrenaline. Our jaws and fists tighten our eyes narrow. Sweat beads at our temples and forehead.

You will very likely find your partner on the battlefield facing the very same Demon of Anger. As you yourself face this demon, it will obstruct you from seeing the fear, hurt and sadness in your partner and it will obstruct them from seeing it in you. If you can slay this demon, toss him to the ground beside you, you will find compassion. You'll see that you are both on this battlefield fighting the same demons.

Unlike many of the other Demons of Change, the Demon of Anger can be tamed to become an ally in our struggle across the battlefield. The Demon of Anger, a sly but fierce protector against perceived injustice, is also a blow horn on the field signaling that something is wrong and in need of corrective action; however if left unattended or ignored this demon can cause great harm.

When not slayed or tamed, the carnivorous Demon of Anger will turn on you and eat away at your heart and soul light without reservation, clouding your insides with darkness. My client Mark was in battle with the Demon of Anger for most of his adult life. Following a tragic football accident where his future as he imagined it was taken away from him, he was filled with anger. He held anger from his relationships with the men in his life and with each subsequent wrongdoing following his accident, the anger would compound. Eventually he was a walking time bomb filled with rage. Anytime he felt injusticed he would immediately react and verbalize his anger. In partnerships he would channel the same aggression and explode when he felt injusticed. Spirit urged him to take a pause and observe the injustice and where it came from. To first seek his partners intent, to ask their intent, to listen. The Demon of Anger obstructs us from seeing the fear, hurt and sadness in our partners, but also obstructs us from *hearing* it. To slay this Demon, you must be willing to see and hear past it. See your partners' experience. Hear them out. You will soften and tame this beast. You will find compassion.

5.05 Exercise

INTENTION: Slay the Demon of Anger

ACTION: The Demon of Anger obstructs us from seeing, hearing and feeling the fear, sadness and hurt in others.

Identify the circumstances that have invited in the Demon of Anger. Find the underlying emotions that are hiding beneath the anger. Dig in, is there hurt here? Fear, sadness, regret? Is it your own, or of someone else's. Find the injustice. In what way do you feel you were harmed or threatened? How would you prefer to have been treated? Find your breath and imagine the aggressor treating you just as you believe you should have been treated. Allow for the feelings of anger to subside. If you are able to share and communicate your desires with the other party, do so once the anger itself has dissipated.

EFFECT: Anger is a great motivator for change. When received and expressed in a constructive manner it encourages us to speak up about an injustice and make a change. Visualizing and feeling into the other party, and visualizing and feeling into the outcome we would prefer or would have preferred, we are able to manifest real change.

the demon of hurt

"Nobody can hurt me without my permission."

MAHATMA GANDHI

THE Demon of Hurt carries a large club and comes in with crippling blows, slowing and prohibiting you from continuing forward. It renders you helpless. Often times you don't see it coming and it leaves you in a wounded heap on the battlefield feeling embarrassed, confused, bruised and offended. This demon moves quickly in and out with a vengeance

My client Aaliyah found a man she connected deeply with. She had a couple of months of deeply passionate loving connection with him, sharing their deepest secrets and desires, dreaming of a future together. Then suddenly one day he vanished. In today's terms... he 'Ghosted'. She was confused and hurt, and she didn't understand what had transpired to make him suddenly leave after all they'd shared. Within a couple of weeks, a friend pointed out a photo of him and a new much younger woman on Instagram. And within a couple of weeks of that she received even more devastating news. She was pregnant. She reached out to him, let him know, and after what had been eight weeks of no response, he responded with a lengthy text explaining how happy he was in his new relationship, and offering to pay for the abortion. Aaliyah was hurt deeply. She went on to terminate the pregnancy and begin her healing process. After two years of healing and deep soul work, she was finally free from the shock and pain of her experience.

The Demon of Hurt often comes in as we are exiting the battlefield. Sometimes the pain of the blow lingers, and like most injuries and wounds, it heals with time. As with the story of Aaliyah, she was able to heal relatively quickly (some men/women will carry this type of trauma for decades or even lifetimes) through intensive soul work and *time*. There were times in her journey where she was keeled over in pain. Times where she had no other escape from the pain than to sleep. The soul work completed after a trauma is akin to an antibiotic ointment, preventing infection, but ultimately the passing of time is needed for complete healing. Eventually, like most wounds, the resulting pain will change form, scab, and heal. And like most wounds, a scar will be left behind.

Hurt is an innate unhappiness or sadness caused by someone's (or our own) words or actions. You can choose to lay in agony on the battlefield, hopelessly gripping onto your wounds, or you can choose to lift yourself up, nurse your wounds, and stagger your way toward the other end of the battlefield.

5.06 Exercise

INTENTION: How to slay the Demon of Hurt

ACTION: Who do I believe I've hurt? Who do I believe has hurt me?

List the first name or few that come to mind and how you may have hurt each other. Sit quietly and examine the dynamics between the two of you. In what way did you or the other feel shocked, stunned, threatened, powerless?

{ Name }, you hurt me when you_____

and I understand that I hurt you when I _____

I made my choice because _____

I know now that you made that choice because_____

I forgive you.

Please forgive me.

EFFECT: Practicing understanding, acceptance and forgiveness continually, your wounds will slowly heal. Because time is needed for hurt to heal, you will need to 're-dress' your wounds until they no longer call for your attention. But know and trust that with continued care and nurturing, your wounds will heal. Your hurt will subside and become scars of your past.

the demon of hurt

"Everything you want is on the other side of fear."
JACK CANFIELD

THE Demon of Fear is the king of all demons. I imagine him to be like Hades, God of the Underworld, controlling the army of the collective of demons we face on the Battlefield to Liberation. His voice is a subtle whisper of fearsome thoughts directly into the backs of our minds. This powerful demon wears many masks. One of the many masks this demon wears is that of a concerned ally. He convinces us that he's acting in our best interest. This can show up in the subtle urgings of our loved ones pushing us to move against our own free will and make choices out of fear. Another mask is that of frightening antagonist and pushes us to turn back running in the opposite direction of where we desire to be. This shows up just as we are about to make a major decision as a mind play-out of the worst possible ways a scenario could unfold This can limit us from moving forward with our hearts desires.

Before I go further about the Demon of Fear, I ask you to ask yourself... Is my fear warranted? Fear is a protective mechanism. What is fear protecting me from? I have worked with women (and men) navigating their way out of abusive relationships with partners suffering from mental illnesses and in these cases the fear is warranted and there are several considerations and measures to be taken to protect the individual and their children. If you are in a relationship where you are living with fear, fear for your own safety or that of your family, seek professional help. Find a local domestic abuse support group or service organization in your area and allow for them to support you in moving forward.

For those of you in comfortable or stable relationships where there is still a pull toward freedom and growth past the limits of the existing relationship (think Chapter One - Illusion of Comfort), the Demon of Fear steps in to keep us from taking risks and reaching for our desires. It keeps us from reaching for our health and wellness goals, career goals, and relationship goals. The Demon of Fear holds us back from taking risks like reaching out to a new friend, trying out that yoga class or applying for that special job. Trying out that new hobby or approaching that cute guy at the bar. When taking that brave step and facing that Demon of Fear, that new friend could be the catalyst to introduce you to your tribe of like-minded people and help you to establish roots in a new town. That yoga class could be the thing that puts you back in touch with the side of yourself that you've been trying to reconnect with. That new job could be the catalyst to catapult you into a high-paid position that awards you the financial freedom you've been seeking. That new hobby could lead to the invention of something desperately needed by society. That cute guy at the bar could be a soul mate, the future father of your children, the one to encourage you to chase after your dreams. You never know the possibilities... do not let fear hold you back.

These 'risks' are all potential catalysts for learning, growth, happiness, bliss, freedom.

What is risk and how does it connect into 'fear'?

Risk is the possibility or *probability of exposure* to danger or pain. Fear is that *unpleasant emotion* caused by the belief that someone or something is a source of danger or pain. With fear, we are inherently less willing to take risks. Locking into the idea of Risk can lock yourself into the belief that you must categorize your possibilities or pathways into better or worse; or safe and dangerous. What if you viewed your options as neither? What if you viewed your options instead as varied pathways to learning and to freedom? What if the possibilities you're weighing against fear are really you weighing your willingness to learn and to be free against those things that hold you back from freedom?

Believing that choosing one option over another as better or worse, or right or wrong, stirs up feelings of fear.

5.07 Exercise

INTENTION: Slay the Demon of Fear

ACTION: Look at each standing decision that you are being called to make in your life right now. Where do you feel paralyzed by fear? Find where you believe the risk or danger is in each decision and create a chart. On the left side of the chart: (Gains) Potential *positive* outcomes. On the right side of the chart: (Dangers) Potential *negative* outcomes. For example: My client Carol in her mid sixties had given up her dreams of having children, traveling, living with joy and peace, during her thirty year marriage with her husband. They slept in separate bedrooms and she spent her days keeping busy so as not to have to return home. Her husband smoked and she hated the smell and began to develop an intolerance, suffering a deep years long cough. Her body began to speak up as it somaticized the pain of her confinement and she began to suffer chronic shoulder pain. Even after surgery the pain persisted. She was on antidepressants to numb the emotional pain and feelings of unrest. I assured her that the message from Spirit was that if she left her marriage the pain would go away and yet she was so engulfed with fear that she would not leave. What was she afraid of? She was afraid that if she left she would not have the means to sustain the lifestyle that she had been living. She was afraid that he would not leave and that if she made the choice the family home, which had been in her family for decades, her family would be disappointed. The perceived probability of exposure to 'danger' or 'pain' for her was living 'without' for a time and/or family upset. The potential 'Gains' for her were freedom from her husband's smoking and negativity, freedom from physical pain and depression, the potential for finding an even *more* loving and supportive partner, and most importantly... peace.

Weigh each of your own 'Dangers' and 'Gains' on paper. As you consider this exit... What are you afraid of? And what could you gain if you leave?.'

EFFECT: Viewing the Dangers beside the Gains, you will likely find that the gains far outweigh any of your fears. Every step of the way, focus on the potential gains. Know that you are worthy. Know and trust in your power and ability to create the life you want, a life full of *exponential* Gains when you move forward again and again without fear. Here you slay and trample that Demon of Fear.

loving the demons of change

"The sooner we heal our traumas, the sooner we liberate ourselves
from the people who hurt us. By hating them, we hold on to them.
We cannot heal."

VIRONIKA TUGALEVA

EACH of the demons you've met on the Battlefield of Change
was Divinely placed on your path on that battlefield to teach you
something about your Self. As you near the end, look back with
gratitude on each experience, battle, encounter and remember
with Love and gratitude the lessons you learned with each.

 He who is devoid of the power to forgive is
devoid of the power to love. There is some
good in the worst of us and some evil in
the best of us. When we discover this, we
are less prone to hate our enemies.

MARTIN LUTHER KING, JR.

6

LEAVING

Leaving

> So you watch yourself about
> complaining. What you're supposed
> to do when you don't like a thing is
> change it. If you can't change it, change
> the way you think about it.
>
> MAYA ANGELOU

resisting change and pracing non-attachment

It can take us weeks, months, or even years to make a decision to leave a relationship. We become attached to our perceived securities and ignore the pull or burning desire to move in the direction of growth. We resist. Think of Resistance as attachment and 'Letting Go' as non-attachment. Think of resistance as you yourself holding tightly onto the reigns of a great ship, moving far in the opposite direction. You're standing in place with your heels digging into the sand, attempting to grasp onto and control and manipulate the direction of this ship. Eventually it's too far gone, and you have no choice but to either allow it to carry you along, or to let go. In both cases, your feet are no longer on the ground, you are no longer in control, you are either moving with the ship, or you have detached yourself from it. This detachment is what many eastern philosophies call 'non-attachment'. You recognize a larger force than yourself, and you no longer resist or grasp. As soon as you stop resisting and grasping and begin practicing non-attachment, you will feel more free. You will feel yourself slowly starting to move in the flow of life. You will see new opportunities opening up for you. You will no longer be digging your feet into the sand, you will be standing a little taller and more erect, and begin to feel more in control,

Why do we resist change?

Thoughts and beliefs that trigger resistance:

☐ fear of the unknown. unpredictability

☐ uncertainty. indecision

☐ fear of failure

☐ lack of confidence

☐ belief in lack of resources

☐ false programming around right vs. wrong

☐ loyalty

☐ perceived obligation

☐ shame

☐ feelings of unworthiness

☐ unprepared = we don't have a plan

Look at the above list and check off which triggers apply to you. The more you check off, the more resistance you are working against to let go and move forward. You will need to release your grip on each of these. At the end of this section I will provide you with positive affirmations for releasing resistance for each of these triggers. But before we get into that, let's look at when it's easier for us to accept change. By understanding when you *can* accept change, we can overlay those ways of thinking with our positive affirmations and your current situation, and begin to release that resistance piece by piece.

So when is it easiest for us to accept change?

Think of the New Year. We know every year, that we will enter a new cycle, we welcome it with open arms at the last stroke of midnight on December 31st each year. We are excited to shed the pains and disappointments of the past year, and excited to welcome the manifestations of our dreams for the coming year. What if we treated the cycles of relationships with this same fervor? Whether it be an ending and beginning of a cycle or pattern of behavior and dynamic within an existing relationship, or the ending and beginning of a completely new relationship; What if we could look forward with excitement at freeing ourselves from the pains and disappointments of a *completed* relationship and excitement for the manifestation of new dreams and experiences to come in a *new* relationship?

Now think of the seasons. Within one cycle of a year, we experience recurrent change every 3 months with the changing of the seasons. Some of us are more comfortable and even need the more drastic change of the season, and some of us prefer the more subtle shifts in seasons. Think of where you fall with your preference for seasonal change and let this be a guide for how you would prefer to navigate change in relationships. If you're okay with that sharp contrast of moderate fall to icy winter, then you may have an easier time letting go of resistance. If you prefer moderate climate year round and could do without the changing of the season, this is a good indicator that you might prefer a very subtle and gradual shift in and out of relationships. Use your knowledge of your preference for navigating the seasons as your guide for navigating change in relationships.

non-attachment: freedom from resistance and freedom from expectation

"Nonresistance, nonjudgement, and non-attachment are the
three aspects of true freedom and enlightened living."
ECKHART TOLLE

With resistance, you attach *(cling)* to who you were in the past and, even as you are growing exponentially into a bigger brighter higher version of your Self, you still cling to your old self. With expectation you attach *(cling)* to the experiences and conditions that you believe will manifest. We are afraid of the void that will be cast in the absence of our partner and so we cling to our relationship with them. We fear not finding someone as intelligent or beautiful, as wealthy, as kind.

When we detach from expectations...

We are not expecting others to love us back, we are not expecting our boss to beg us to stay, and we are not expecting our ex-lover to want to maintain friendship with us. We are not expecting anything. We are standing in our own power and beginning to hand over those reigns of control to the Universe to work things out in better ways than you could've imagined. But first, you have to 'let go' and hand over the reigns. *You* have to let go.

6.01 Exercise

INTENTION: Practicing Letting Go & Non-Attachment.

ACTION: If you are ready to attempt to let go of your past, the first step is to recognize what you are hanging onto. Sit and ask yourself... what am I clinging to? What am I attached to? Set intention to let go. Affirm out loud, as if in conversation with yourself or another person, that you desire to let go.

Examine the list of resistance triggers and for each that you feel resonant, affirm the following:

(see next page)

86

6.01 Exercise (cont.)

RESISTANCE TRIGGERING THOUGHT	RESISTANCE CANCELING AFFIRMATION
fear of the unknown	"I fearlessly take one step at a time into the unknown."
unprepared = I don't have a plan	"I trust in the guidance of my heart and intuition."
uncertainty, indecision	"I make choices for my highest good and know that beacause of this all is well."
fear of failure	"There is no failure in effort. I succeed with every effort I put forth."
lack of confidence	"I have the power to make my dreams a reality."
belief in lack of resources	"I am supplied for every day."
false programming around right vs. wrong	"There is no wrong when I move from the heart."
loyalty	"I let go at the right time and in the right way."
preceived obligation	"I give my best, and I let go of the rest."
shame	"My heart is good and kind."
feelings of unworthiness	"I am worthy of Divine Love and Favor."

EFFECT: Letting go is a practice. It takes consistent conscientious intention and action. The simple action of affirming out loud your intention to let go, and affirming out loud the trigger canceling affirmations, will begin to reprogram your mind into a state of less resistance and greater sense of worthiness.

What if I can't let go?

Sometimes the reigns are ripped from our grips and we come to an uncomfortable place where the decision to let go is made for us... initiated by a natural ending, a tragedy or the other party in the relationship. It could be a work lay-off. An affair. Death. In these cases, the actual *feeling* of letting go is more out of range and must catch up with the reality that a separation has been forced.

As incomprehensible as it may seem, these moments are opportunities for both parties to grow. One party may not be ready for that growth and we have free will in each moment to make a conscious choice to remain or to move forward. We are living in such a loving Universe that no matter what choice we make, we will always be held, loved and supported in our attempts to live, love and learn. Waiting for the decision to be made for us places us into a state of limbo that can last months, years, decades. Waiting for your boss to let you go, for your lover to end things, for your partner to die, you postpone your own freedom and joy, and oftentimes the body will cry out for you to take action. Whether it be chronic pain, illness, depression, anxiety or other, your body will speak. Your 'waiting' prohibits you from leaving with the closure that would put your heart to rest and inhibits our soul's opportunity to fully leave with love.

Why Don't We Leave

Those who do not move, do not notice their chains.
ROSA LUXEMBURG

Ultimately, if no harm is coming to anyone involved, there is no right or wrong as to why or how long you should stay in a relationship. Your heart is your clearest guide for when and whether you should stay or go. People stay in relationships for a multitude of reasons. Common reasons we don't leave relationships or hold on too long:

1. We are comfortable
2. We fear we cannot do better
3. We do not want to hurt the other party
4. We have kids
5. We are loyal

we are comfortable

Relationships, especially those of co-dependence where one or both partners come to rely on each other for all of their decision-making and general survival, can create the illusion of comfort being dependent on the other party. In a job, you could be satisfied with your salary and workload but know that your soul is not being fed and nourished in the way that it most desires to be. It's like a diet of canned tuna on white bread where you could certainly go on living with this diet, but your physical body is begging for more nutrients. In my own relationship, comfort showed up as living with my best friend, financial security, shared finances, shared homeownership, predictability... But my soul was crying out for deeper nourishment. I needed partnership, I needed understanding, I needed physical touch, eventually my needs overrode the existing comforts. I set out to conquer that Demon of Ambivalence and feed my soul.

we fear we cannot do better

Many people come to a point in their lives and within their relationships where they experience low self-worth and a loss of self-confidence. This applies to romantic relationships, coworkers, friendships, and family. We forget our own beauty and value and fear we can do no better.

Slay that Demon of Fear!

If you are confronting this block, go back and complete or review the exercise in self-value in the Chapter One section on Illusion of Rejection.

we do not want to hurt the other party

When we love and care for someone, regardless if we want to remain in a committed relationship with them, we don't want to hurt them. When you believe that your choice to leave a relationship will disappoint, offend, hurt, crush another person, you step into a face-up with the Demon of Guilt. Conquer that Demon of guilt and remember that you've both experienced hurt in some way. Keep your intention for compassion and kindness and this momentary hurt could be one of the most powerful catalysts for both yourself and the other person involved.

we have kids

Our love for our children makes us most vulnerable to the Demon of Denial. In marriages and committed partnerships where children are involved, some individuals convince them that things aren't so bad, that they can wait until the children are older, and they convince themselves that the children need their parents to stay together. Later when they're older, many children of divorced parents come back and express that they wished their parents would've separated sooner. Children and teens, no matter their age, are extremely intuitive and sensitive to their parents' emotional states. They can feel when a parent is unhappy, resentful, or emotionally detached. The belief that you need to stay together for your children can hold you hostage in these emotional states.

we are loyal

In my battle with the Demon of Guilt, during my transition from leaving the group holistic practice and opening my own studio, I battled my own sense of loyalty. It propagated the guilt. I felt loyal to the name and to the amazing team of practitioners that had welcomed me in with open arms. I felt such a sense of loyalty that I had difficulty making the decision to follow my heart. In the end, the heart won. Loyalty can enslave you into situations and relationships you have outgrown. See Chapter Eight Section - Taking Space From Family Members for more on loyalty.

And of course... Those Seven Demons of Change are all reasons we don't leave!

Why Do We Leave

> Has this world been so kind to you that you
> should leave with regrets? There are better
> things ahead than we leave behind.
>
> C.S. LEWIS

Although some relationships end on positive terms or of mutual understanding, many end as the result of some lasting discomfort. Reasons why we *do* consider leaving any and all relationships, be it romantic, professional, platonic or familial:

1. Your soul is not being fed. Instead it is being depleted.
2. You are resentful
3. Your relationship is toxic or abusive
4. Your desire for spiritual conquest
5. You desire to explore or be in other Relationships

your soul is not being fed. instead it is being depleted.

You'll hear me say it many times in this book and in person... our cumulative experience here is to experience the giving and receiving of love. Resting too long in a space of deficiency, especially in relationships, is detrimental to your overall wellness and growth.

When your soul is not being fed within your relationships, when you're feeling empty and stagnant and the feelings of love have dissipated, when you are tired and uninspired in your relationship... Your soul is not being fed. The soul is fed by the giving and receiving of service, inspiration, love, affection, laughter, even pain if worked through properly. If you are in a relationship where you are constantly finding yourself giving and not receiving...whether by your own choosing or by your partner's lack of ability to give... then the time may be presenting itself for you to make change.

The first step needn't be right out of the relationship (unless you choose that), but it can be stating clearly your expectation. State your need. Verbally articulate to your partner what love needs are not being met in your relationship, and ask if they believe they can fulfill those needs.

By doing the necessary work to recognize your own value, releasing your own blocks to love and vulnerability, being generous with your love and stating your love needs, you allow yourself to get into the flow of giving and receiving.

If you are not blocking yourself from receiving and you are in relationship with someone who needs to learn to proportionately give, than you still have options before leaving the relationship (unless you're already ready to leave). You can try couples counseling, reading supportive books together like *The Five Love Languages*, which teaches the art of tuning into your partners needs by understanding their language for giving and receiving love. You can have open honest conversations with your partner about your needs and set clear expectations and parameters for measure. Regardless of if you are reviewing a relationship with a lover, a family member or a friend, liken this to having an employee and letting them know what you expect out of them and when. Be as generous as you want to be but give them a timeline. This is your free will, you can choose to give a week or give a decade.

Setting clear expectations and measures sets you both up for growth and success in or out of this relationship.

you are resentful

You're carrying the bitterness of perceived wrongdoing of your partner, everywhere. You obsess or are easily triggered by their behaviors. They begin to view you as a nag or nitpick and you both become more and more resentful. Everything your partner does drives you crazy. You feel like a different, lesser version of your Self when with them.

Again we begin within and ask those enlightening questions... What is it within me that gets so shaken and stirred by my partner's actions? Do I have needs that are not being met that are prohibiting me from seeing my partners' light?

Our bodies undergo a gazillion physical, emotional and hormonal changes over the course of our lives. When we are not eating properly, when we are not caring for ourselves, when we feel unsexy, under these conditions and heightened emotions we sometimes stop loving and maybe even start *hating* ourselves...and then we begin to hate our partners. This pattern can apply to men and women who've just had children. It could apply to the employee that works so hard by their desk side, barely getting up for a break, working such long hours that they don't leave time for friendships and self-care activities. This employee can begin to hate their job and everyone in it.

Wherever your resentment lies, first look inward and begin with making time and space for your Self. Take care of yourself. Find joy in your personal life. If this relationship is intended to withstand the tests of your resentments, these signals to take some time and care for your Self, then it will withstand. Resentment is not always a deal breaker in relationships, but resentment held without personal responsibility and concerted effort to make change usually results in an ending of the relationship as it was.

your relationship is toxic or abusive

At the point when a relationship becomes toxic or abusive, bringing you harm and continued suffering, than you've reached that handoff point to where one or both parties should step out of the relationship and onto varying paths of growth and evolution. We can review the relationship and its lessons, and quickly free ourselves from karmic ties. Even with forgiveness the energy of toxicity and abuse is extremely difficult to release on both ends. The feelings of unworthiness and mistrust within them in the presence of one another and they unconsciously continually invite the Demon of Guilt back in. See Chapter Nine section Cord Cutting for more practices in how to free yourself from the demons of your past.

you desire for spiritual conquest

When I was in college and I first learned the story of the Buddha who felt a call onto his spiritual journey and left behind his wife and child in spiritual conquest, I could not fathom how he or any other parent could leave their partner and child for a spiritual conquest, traveling to faraway lands seeking spiritual knowledge and enlightenment. It wasn't until after I'd had children and divorced, and witnessed firsthand how my balance and spiritual understandings brought such peace and wisdom into my home environment with my children. Than I understood. Similarly, men and women leave their partners and families everyday to serve their countries and the "greater good" in service organizations like the military and Peace corps.

If you're feeling the call to higher education, spiritual study or service... listen. Make your best effort to make change with love and compassion with as minimal harm to others as possible.

you desire to explore or be in other relationships

When you've outgrown clothing or shoes, you look for new ones that accomodate the new 'you'. Relationships can be similar in that when the time comes for transitioning out of a relationship that we've outgrown, we will commonly begin to feel sparks of desire for relating with others. A feeling deep inside ignites your attraction to another person. Those butterflies in your gut start swirling when you see someone attractive and your mind starts imagining the possibilities. You might find yourself having deep conversations with others and wondering why you can't have this with your partner. Ask yourself, am I okay with this? These are early indicators of the time for transition coming near.

However, transition doesn't necessarily mean out of the existing relationship entirely, but it might signal the need for transition into a new way of relating. Start by asking yourself as you explore the possibilities of relationship - Could I have this with my partner? If you answer yes, then begin with meditating/praying and asking Spirit "What is this first step that I need to take in order to manifest this within my relationship?" Listen and follow and watch the magic unfold. If your answer is no, and you would rather leave your relationship to explore other possibilities, your time to consider leaving this relationship has arrived.

7

VISIONS OF A
BETTER FUTURE

Visions of a Better Future

It is not actual suffering but the taste
of better things which excites people
to revolt.

ERIC HOFFER

What is it that finally moves us to make some form of change to our position in our relationships? Suffering certainly does. But even in the absence of suffering and within the presence of comfort and contentment there is commonly a vision of something 'better' that presents itself. My client Lisa came to me with feelings of depression. She'd done some work on her Self for about a year, made a major transformation of her health and wellness, and still suffered these lows. During one session, she described that although she was content in her marriage, she was having visions of another man. Her subconscious mind was fully aware that there was something more and that it was not there in that seemingly perfect moment. She went on to confess a recurring vision that she'd had for months. She said that she would see herself waking up in her same house, with pictures on the walls, but the pictures on the walls were herself with another man. In this vision, she would walk through the house quietly and find herself sitting to a perfectly made cup of coffee with a man who she could not identify. This was in stark contrast to her experience with her husband. She didn't know it until then, but this was what her soul was calling out for. Lisa took her visions to heart, connected more and more into her intuition through meditation and yoga practice, and things in her life flowed beautifully and quickly in the direction of positive change. She completed her doctorate, moved into her own place, and after about 6 months came to me with big news. She was engaged. She'd met the man from her visions, they'd quickly fallen in love, she received a job offer in his town, found a new place in that town. She came to me after and said that her new fiancée, was the man she'd seen in her previous visions, while she was still married. It was as if her subconscious and her spirit team were nudging her forward with reassurance that there would be someone there just around the bend. It was scary to follow those nudges and make that final decision to leave her marriage, but today Lisa is so happy and at peace with her new love, new job, new town.

These visions are gifts from our Higher Selves. Clues in this journey of life and love, urging us on into a more evolved experience in love. Desire shows up as a signal of the possibility for achieving, acquiring or attracting something of value into our lives. That which we value shifts and evolves over time, just as we do. Sometimes we don't see the vision or the signs until that new desire has already fully manifested itself in our lives. This can often lead to that overlap in transition from one 'teacher' to another... what we call infidelity in our culture.

exits and infidelity

Where the cracks in the foundation of your relationship lie, this is where the offerings of someone or something new will enter.

We can turn to many outside sources for comfort and relief when we are not receiving what we need from our partners or providing it for ourselves. Sometimes we turn to positive sources and other times we can turn to harmful sources of comfort and relief. Depending on where the crack lies in your foundation, you or your partner might turn to drugs and alcohol, your work, gambling, the gym... Or you might turn to another person. Infidelity in relationships occurs when we enter into a romantic or sexual relationship with someone other than our monogamous partner. In new polyamorous relationships, occurrence of infidelity is much lower because these relationships are generally based on the premise of openness and truthfulness. In a committed relationship, infidelity occurs when one partner encounters what presents as a new or 'better' opportunity. Just as with Hannah and her visions, sometimes the new opportunity or person is in fact a better fit, a deeper connection, or more in alignment with the person they've become. That doesn't make it any less painful to accept. The exit of a loved one into the arms of another is one of the most painful blows our ego will ever suffer. If your soul has elected to experience either side of this, you are experiencing an elevated lesson in love, ego and forgiveness.

My client Rob sat teary eyed in my chair as he explained how much he loved his wife, how she was an amazing woman, incredible mother, his best friend... But he just wasn't sexually attracted to her. He could not have sex with her. He was feeling tempted from women in his workplace and out in his work travels, and doing his best to combat his own desires... But he was suffering. As I'll say again and again in this book, this universe is a kind one and suffering is only here to move us. In his case, it was a karmic call for him to make a choice or make a sacrifice. And as many men and women choose in this life, he chose to wait until his children were of college age before making any decision to leave his wife. However here, I will also remind you, what I hear from many of the college-aged children of parents who waited for them to graduate, and that is they wish their parents would've separated sooner. These adult children have shared with me time and time again that they could feel their parents' sadness and depression, they could feel their separateness, and they share that all they would want is for both parents to be happy. For my client Rob, the guidance from Spirit that came through in our work together, was for him to open up an honest line of communication with his wife. To consciously and kindly share his feelings and allow her the opportunity to process through some of it with him. Spirit also shared with him that he could open up a discussion with his wife about taking a lover. The first time I heard the message from Spirit encouraging someone to consider taking a lover, I was baffled. I thought certainly I can't be hearing this correctly, and I couldn't bring myself to share that message. But I have made a commitment with the Spirit world, and that is to share openly and honestly the messages that I receive as they come. After that first time, I've since worked with many couples and individuals where messages came through in support of the idea of taking a lover.

We always have free will, and should you not feel comfortable with the idea of taking a lover, then you may not be ready for it. My deepest hope with sharing these stories in this small section of this book, is that you might open up your heart to hear your partner out. Listen to their needs. Share your own. We are growing and evolving in consciousness and should you agree to be open to exploration of openness in your relationship, you both may find a deeper sense of liberation.

A similar message came through for my client Vanessa who was in a committed relationship with a wealthy and much older partner. He provided a home and security, however he was not able to meet her needs for passion and depth of connection. They had a sweet relationship, very much a father-daughter dynamic, and she loved him very much but she was suffering from loneliness and depression. She was beginning to resent him and with that resentment she was feeling more and more disconnected from her naturally loving and bright self. The message from Spirit was for her to consider having an open conversation with her partner to discuss her unmet needs and her desire to maintain their relationship and to have her needs met. Spirit shared that if she were to take a lover and have her needs for passion met she would be freed of the resentment and would again shine brightly as she had before.

In our culture, we've been taught, programmed and conditioned through our families, churches, communities and the media, to believe that relationships must 'look' a certain way. But what we haven't been taught, is how to create and build relationship structures that work for our unique and individual selves. We are in a time when we have the opportunity to be teachers for one another and learn new ways of relating in order to transcend the old. We can only reach this point through exploration and open honest dialogue with our partners. By slowly breaking down the barriers of fear and judgment of what's new and different from what we were taught, we can create a safe space for our partners to express and articulate their needs, and help one another to build a new foundation based on honesty and openness.

If you have a partner that has 'cheated', first I encourage you to let go of the word 'cheated' and the storyline and replace it now by acknowledging that they were 'dishonest'. Then I encourage you to dig in and ask your Self, why were they dishonest? What were they afraid of? What needs did they have that were either not expressed or not understood?

Dishonesty enters in with the Demon of Fear. Many find themselves in positions where they fear sharing their needs and experiences for fear of hurting another, for fear of losing your partner, privileges or children, for fear of the unknown.

In life there are many truths and in infidelity there are many more. In order to heal the energy of infidelity, Spirit guides us to review the many truths hidden beneath the illusions and release ourselves from them all. Ultimately, the truths don't matter. Forgiveness matters. And moving forward with love matters. For those of you thinking "there is no way I'm moving forward with love for this person that hurt me" - Spirit urges you to be willing to move forward with love for your Self and others. On the receiving or defending end of infidelity, you might close your heart off seeking to protect it from further hurt and disappointment. A closed heart that results from this hurt prohibits you from moving forward with love for your Self and others.

You can begin to open your heart during or after dealing with dishonesty and/or infidelity by a compassionate review of your partners' needs and fears.

Forgiveness

> The more difficult it is to forgive
> someone the greater the opportunity
> for spiritual growth.
>
> GABRIELLE BERNSTEIN

FORGIVENESS is recognizing where the needs of another were not met. When we are able to recognize where someone else's needs being unmet led to harmful or hurtful actions, we are able to compassionately let go of the negative feelings associated with the choices made as a result. In releasing all of the blocks of our own ego and our own stories, we can hear and see and feel into the stories of others with compassion and deep within that recognition we find forgiveness. Recognition is not equal to understanding. Spirit asks that we see the immediate walls that come up for us when the request or intention for 'understanding' is triggered. We think "no, I can't have understanding for that terrible act of harm that this individual committed". In those moments, we are placing ourselves in the role of judge. We think we know how to protect ourselves and others from possible hurt, anguish or disappointment triggered by this situation. However when we simply *agree to witness as an observer* and recognize their individual story, we unintentionally open a tiny space for understanding to sift in. In that space, there is room for above all things... forgiveness.

Angelica's mother was a teenage mother who gave her up for

adoption when she was born. When Angelica reached grade school her young birth mother, married and with a new child of her own, decided that she was ready to take on motherhood with the daughter she'd given up. Angelica was returned to her birth mother and under her care suffered tremendous abuse and trauma for several years and was eventually returned to the safety and care her adopted mother. In adulthood, Angelica was able to consciously and compassionately review the cycle of mental illness and abuse that her birth mother had suffered in order to find forgiveness and to let go. Through journaling exercises, dream work, regression therapy, soul retrieval work, she was able to heal herself and recognize where her birth mothers' needs were unmet thus leading to the cycle of abuse. She was able to release the feelings of hurt, betrayal and hate that she'd harbored most of her life.

This was where she found forgiveness.

Many times when we leave relationships there are negative feelings of hurt, sadness, betrayal, and/or victimization. If we can allow ourselves a moment (whether that moment be weeks, months, or years) to be with those feelings, to fully experience them, then our time comes to free ourselves of this karma. Remember karma? The belief in the flow of energy from one source to another in a constant striving attempt to be in balance. Our work is to allow that energy to flow. When we hold the negative energy and feelings of an experience, we are not allowing for that energy to flow and be released for balancing. We do not need to be the ones to balance this energy. The rules of this Universe hold that karma will strive to balance itself. It wants to balance itself. On a soul-level, we do take an active role as co-creators in the balancing of karma; however if we don't trust in this Universe to be a much wiser force than ourselves, we are limiting ourselves from learning the lessons within the experience.

Forgiveness is recognizing where the needs of another were not met and letting go of the negative feelings associated with the choices made as a result of their unmet needs. Forgiveness frees you up from the negative feelings and allows you to move forward with a healed and open heart. Forgiveness is where we are when we finally leave with love.

7.01 Exercise

INTENTION: Review of partners' unmet needs and fears

ACTION: Sit with a journal in hand, low lighting and a candle if possible. Create as sacred a space as you can so that you can attempt to connect with your partner or ex-partner on a soul level across any distance. First coming into a meditative position, deepening your breathe, tuning into your heart and with each out breath imagining exhaling out anger, inhaling in calm. Continue for a few breaths until you feel you've created a little space for openness. Once you've done so, begin to imagine that this person is actually sitting directly across from you. Imagine their face and features, their posture, expression, and tune into their energy. Begin to inquire why they were dishonest with you. What were their unmet needs? Allow answers to come naturally and without attachment to what you 'think' they would say or feel. Keep your mind and heart wide open while you tune into their truths. Ask your partner (or ex-partner) what they were afraid of?

EFFECT: In looking at the unmet needs of your partner and understanding their fears, we can slowly begin to find compassion and heal the hurt in our hearts left behind by dishonesty, infidelity, abandonment and any other hurts.

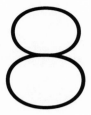

HOW TO LEAVE

How To Leave

 The only thing more unthinkable than leaving was staying; the only thing more impossible than staying was leaving.

ELIZABETH GILBERT

AFTER a period of being in relationship with another person, group or organization, you may choose to conclude the relationship. In our culture when we desire to part ways or leave a relationship with a lover, we often call it a 'break-up' or separation. The words surrounding 'break-up' and separation can trigger heightened emotion. Before you go deep into articulating your desires for conclusion to your partner, I urge you to review the feelings invoked by and develop your own language surrounding the ending of your relationship. Words carry power. Consider what it is that you want and develop your own language for this ending.

Take a moment to sit with the word '*Break*' and the following words and their definitions from Merriam Webster's Dictionary. Notice if it holds negative or positive connotations. There are two major distinct meanings of this word: noun and verb.

VERB

\'brāk \ broke\ 'brōk \; broken\ 'brō-kən \; breaking

: to end a relationship, connection, or agreement —usually used with or from

1. separate or cause to separate into pieces as a result of a blow,

shock, or strain.
synonyms: shatter, smash, crack, snap, fracture, fragment, splinter,
fall to bits, fall to pieces

NOUN

1. an interruption of continuity or uniformity.
synonyms: interruption, interval, gap, hiatus;

2. a pause in work or during an activity or event.
synonyms: rest, respite, recess

: to cause an open wound in : RUPTURE
break the skin

: to make ineffective as a binding force
break the spell

POSITIVE CONNOTATIONS OF THE WORD

: to find an explanation or solution for : SOLVE
the detective broke the case

break even
: to achieve a balance

break free
: to get away by overcoming restraints or constraints

break ground
1 : to begin construction

ADDITIONAL SYNONYMS

disassociate, disconnect, disjoin, disjoint, dissever, dissociate, dis-
unite, divide, divorce, part, ramify, resolve, separate, sever, split, sun-
der, uncouple, unlink, unyoke

8.01 Exercise

INTENTION: Mindful Language: Get clear on your intentions for the conclusion of this relationship.

ACTION: Are you seeking temporary suspension, permanent ending, to pause and take a breather, interrupt an unhealthy pattern, detach, disconnect, separate, divorce, uncouple, break free? Whether you've already left or are contemplating leaving, write a one-page letter to whomever you seek to disconnect from, mindfully expressing the 'honest action' that you are seeking to take and what you are hoping to gain by taking that action. Read and re-write this letter again and again until you feel clear.

EFFECT: This letter is solely to help you to get clear on your intentions for concluding this relationship. When the 'right' time is presented (Keep reading for Chapter 8 section on Timing), you will have the mindful language to use to communicate and articulate your needs clearly to your partner. This is a helpful exercise to do at any point in a relationship when you are feeling the need for change or conclusion.

If you find it particularly difficult weighing this decision and you've completed the pros and cons chart exercise, begin to call on your helping spirits to lovingly guide you through the transition.

deadlines and ultimatums

Is a breakup or separation what you truly desire?

A friend once asked me "How did you know you were sure you wanted to leave?" I responded, "I didn't know. I don't think you ever 'know.' I set a deadline. I provided an ultimatum. If certain behaviors and patterns hadn't changed by that deadline, I would leave. The deadline came, and so I followed through with my promised action." The difference between an ultimatum and a deadline is plan and action. With a deadline you set a date for completion of task or fulfillment of duty. *I need you to become a contributing partner in this household by the end of this year.* With an ultimatum you set an outcome or condition for completion. *If you don't become a contributing partner in this household by the end of this year, this marriage is over.* As with most plans, if you don't set a date, you are less likely to follow through.

If you are considering ending a relationship but open to a final attempt at recovery, give your partner (or friend, colleague, whomever) specific measures to be met. State your measures, set a deadline, and stick with it. Even if you decide to cycle back around and give the relationship another try, chances are it will be more successful after you've made your measures known and demonstrated actual repercussions.

Was I 100% certain and without doubt after making my decision to end my marriage... No. We all are in a constant state of co-creation with this Universe, it's nearly impossible to have complete certainty about our futures. Because of everyone's ability to exercise free will there is no real certainty about anything. It's all playing out live, moment to moment. You can have confidence in your decision... Probabilities can run high for certain outcomes, but still, they are not certain.

8.02 Exercise

INTENTION: Setting a deadline and an ultimatum

ACTION: Are you ready to make a decision? What change are you seeking in your relationship? Instead of fixating on whether or not you are 'certain,' pay attention to where you feel yourself leaning. Are you already leaning toward leaving? Or are you leaning toward attempting to recover your relationship? Set a deadline for whatever action it is that you would like to take. Clarify the terms of your ultimatum and share them with your partner.

EFFECT: With a deadline and clear terms of your ultimatum, you will be creating momentum for both your partner and yourself to make actual change.

making a plan

Once you've set a date and terms of your ultimatum, begin to create a mindful plan for how you will move forward after your given deadline. Consider the conditions that you feel to be fair and kind to yourself and the other party. Being fair and kind is very difficult if you are angry or emotional. By planning in advance, before you reach the deadline, you are taking many of these considerations into account before emotions run high. A prenuptial is a solid example of a written plan for conditions to follow in the event that a marriage does not leave. Married or not, you can set terms for how you will proceed forward following the conclusion of a relationship and it will save everyone involved the struggle of having to figure it out later when emotions are high.

A Compassionate Agreement, would be any agreement made between you and the other person involved, where you both agree to take each other's best interest into account. Compassion for one another, you make decisions for moving forward, boundaries, division of assets, based on mutual agreement and least harm to one another.

8.03 Exercise

INTENTION: Build Compassionate Agreements early on to minimize stress of decision making when emotions are high

ACTION: List all of the loose ends and considerations that would need to be tied up and taken into account upon or prior to leaving the relationship. Questions to ask and considerations to take into account:

- How will we communicate? How often? In what capacity?
- What boundaries do I need to maintain?
- Will we maintain a friendship? A sexual relationship?
- Will we continue to support one another? emotionally? financially?

- If you share belongings... Who will take what? What will you take with you?
- If you live together... Where will you live?
- Are you under a lease? Could you make a compassionate agreement to find someone to take your place or sublet?
- Are you in debt to this person or organization? Can you develop a plan for repayment? would it require you to continue under this relationship or could you make a compassionate agreement to repay your debt over a set time period?
- Consider other financial implications... Retirement funds, insurance beneficiaries. If you are planning a divorce, many of these will need to be considered as a part of your official separation agreement.
- Are there kids involved or is your partner expecting? If there are kids involved... How will we handle the kids? Could you make a compassionate agreement outlining how you will support them following your transition?

Any other questions that arise, sit with them, build yourself a plan and begin to craft a Compassionate Agreement you can share with your partner.

EFFECT: Once you've worked through some of the above scenarios in your mind, plan a sit down with your partner. Decide whether you will have the conversation in person or over the phone. Would you prefer a public place or private? If you allow yourself to mindfully plan and execute this conversation before resentments have built up within the relationship, you will both walk away in a more positive light than had you not.

grace

Remember with gratitude the gifts of this relationship. Even in the most heated of moments surrounding the ending of a relationship, you can pause and gain understanding into the hurt of the other party. Do your best to hold gratitude for the many lessons shared during this relationship. If the decision to end is not a shared decision, it is very easy for one or both parties to end up feeling defensive and weaving and replaying stories of blame and wrongdoing. To shift out of that energy and leave with grace, avoid falling into the trap of feeling that you have to defend yourself. Ignore the insults, attacks, rumors and rants and quietly (in your mind or in your journal) thank the other party for all that they've shared, taught and brought into your life and walk away. Let yourself genuinely feel the goodness of your time together. Leaving a relationship doesn't have to be meddled with negativity and complaint.

Grace also means releasing your ego from involvement with any insults or attacks by the other party who may be reacting out of hurt. Walking away with grace and dignity if and when the attacks become abusive in any way. Today, that means not responding, gracefully blocking the calls or social media accounts of the other party. Physically removing yourself from scenes and settings where the attacks are likely to unfold. Recognize where their attacks are coming from and don't take their words and actions personally.

timing

Once you've made the decision to leave a relationship, you will likely sit with the decision for a while. Depending on the length of the relationship this stewing time can range from a few months to a few years. Be gentle with yourself no matter how long you need to sit with the decision, but do yourself a favor and don't wait too long. You'll know it's too long when the Demons of Change start rolling in in packs. You'll find them stacking up on top of you, Fear, Anger, Guilt, and know that it's time to break free.

Timing is critical.

I had a dream once that I was a man leaving a party with

another man. As we were driving we realized that we had brought along the dead body of another man from the party. In our trunk. As we're driving I'm saying to the other man, why did we bring this dead man's body with us? Now it's going to look like we killed him.

We had the added weight now of figuring out how to dispose of this dead body gracefully and with respect, but now we're added in layers of fear and regret. Would the cops pull us over and think that we had killed this man?

This dream was a brutally direct message from my subconscious that my marriage was 'dead' and that if I moved forward into a relationship with another man without leaving it behind, I would be carrying the dead weight of my marriage forward with me. It was a message urging me to be mindful in how I left and to do so with grace and respect.

Timing can be the determining factor in whether this separation will end amicably. In some cases, no matter what you do it will not end amicably... But still be mindful with your timing. Will you need to make this break around the holidays, just after a vacation, right before a wedding or birth of a child? Sometimes the kindest thing we can do for another person, is patiently set aside our desires for the right timing. If you find yourself desiring to end a relationship at an inopportune time, ask yourself: "When would be the least harmful moment for both of us?" You need not completely sacrifice your own desires, but the difference in days, weeks or months could entirely shift the energy of the separation. This also works in the reverse of patience in that you may find yourself feeling a push to make the break quickly. Spirit may be lining you up for new opportunity and encouraging you to create space.

Listen to those nudges inside of you that quietly (and sometimes loudly) encourage you to wait or 'act now!'. You'll feel it like a burning desire or firm push from within, a strong pull in a new direction, recurrent thoughts of a direction or action you should take. Recurring dreams. Separate out the Demons from the supportive nudges by recognizing thoughts that are based in fear, fueled by anger or holding you locked in by guilt. A supportive nudge will push you in the direction of your Highest good. Make your best attempt to time your exit mindfully with as minimal harm to others *and your Self.*

This is where we set a final intention to separate in a way that is mindful and compassionate with the least harm done.

walking away from friendships

FRIENDS are earth angels or soul mates (See Chapter Two - Understanding Soul Relationships) here to walk us through various phases of our lives. Some will be with us through most of our lives, from birth on, and others will step in in key phases of your and their lives. Some friendships take momentary breaks while the two of you are experiencing life respectively. Emotionally, years or even decades away from an old friend can feel as if no time has passed at all. If you find yourself within a break in friendship, allow that space for your friend and yourself to grow and experience life independently for a moment and trust that the love will sustain. Not allowing this space can have detrimental effects - resentments, mistrust, and claustrophobia.. If you are in need of space within a friendship and it is not naturally unfolding, it can be a gift to the friendship to articulate your needs. Sometimes with more evolved friendships, this is not necessary, but if you sense the need to express your desire for space, do so lovingly and directly.

taking space from family members

Ever wonder where that old saying 'blood runs thicker than water" originated from? This famous old English proverb that means that family relations and bonds are deeper and more long-lasting than any other relationships, has been traced back to the thirteenth century Reinhart Fuchs manuscript in German. "ouch hoer ich sagen, das sippe blŭt von wazzere niht verdirbet" (lines 265-266). In English it was translated to, *"I also hear it said, kin-blood is not spoiled by water."*

In this translation the 'water' spoken of is the sea. Thus declaring that kin and familial relationships and ties could not be 'spoiled' or broken by the distance across the sea.

This phrase is used (and misused) within families and organizations to appeal to the loyalty of an individual and to enforce guilt. Growing up, I heard this phrase misused to proclaim that family 'blood' was stronger and deeper than friends and others outside the family 'water'. The appeal to loyalty is not only used in families, but in military service, political campaign and other forms of organizational structure. I never connected with this phrase and wondered why. As I evolved and grew to develop my own understanding of our existence across time, I came to understand and believe that we have all been 'blood' family in one lifetime or another. Someone who is your best friend in this life was very likely your sibling in a past life, and your soul likely still carries the soul connection and deep seated loyalties of that past life kinship.

Loyalty, our devotion and faithfulness to our nation, family group, organization, or to an individual, is one of the strongest forces that holds us hostage in past and present relationships. If you feel stressed when a friend or family member expresses a need to you, and you feel as if you can't say no, but have no choice... You are a hostage to your loyalty. If you can't leave your home or town or job because of the disappointment you believe it will bring upon your family (or partner, business or organization)... You are a hostage to your loyalty. Give yourself permission to take some self-loving space from family relationships that are holding you hostage and causing you suffering and discomfort.

leaving a job

My client Amanda was pretty over her job. She was tired of being taken advantage of by her boss, tired of the disorganization, and the fear that the company might go under at any moment. Overtime, indifference and complacency crept in and she came to that point where she said she just didn't care anymore. She was just collecting her check. Her angels and spirit guides showed up to tell her that it was totally okay to be feeling the way that she was...but that they could help her most if she at least started to think about what she could do next if she were to leave her job. They asked that she try to be compassionate to her boss. They expressed that they knew it would be difficult to feel compassion for him, but that all she had to do was ask for help.

I recommended her to connect with the Goddess Kuan Yin.

Amanda's spirit guides shared that, if she were to be compassionate in the workplace, to continue to do her best, and to have an idea of what she'd like to do next. Not only could they {her own spirit guides} help her, but other people on Earth and in her social circles would want to help her. Miracles would happen. When you find yourself jaded as you contemplate leaving a job or organization, set an intention to leave on a high note. Reach out to the Divine for help with working things out in the most positive miraculous way possible. Stay positive and watch magic happen.

separation and divorce

"The only way to get over a death is by seeing it as a life completed,
instead of a life interrupted."

ANONYMOUS

DIVORCE is often compared to death and the loss of a loved one, but there are many deaths that occur before, during and following a separation and divorce. The first death is the hope that the relationship would survive. Then follows the death of the Illusions of Comfort and Security. See the death of the family structure as it was, the death of friendships, and finally the death of the ego. At one point or another, both parties in the relationship are likely to experience some soul loss and death of ego.

Divorce is a collection of deaths, but more importantly that collection of 'deaths' is a completion of a life cycle. After my period of mourning the death of my marriage, Spirit took me back to an early memory of my husband and I on one of our first dates. I saw the beauty in his face, the excitement, and the love. I was urged to leave with that memory and those feelings of love intact. We'd completed a beautiful cycle of life and love together. We'd traveled, played, explored, served, birthed beautiful babies and grown. As we grew in different directions, our time had come to release our grip on one another and continue forward on our individual paths. Was I certain that I wanted to let go? No. But in the final moments, the resentments that built up, the callusing from holding on too tight to a partner that was not moving in my same direction, became too painful. It wasn't that I wanted to let go, but I had to. The release wasn't easy. Even after I made my decision to separate, I gripped tightly for another six months following our separation as I battled those Demons on the Battlefield of Change.

Following a divorce, we naturally experience a period of grief quite parallel to that of the loss of a close family member, a best friend. For many, this is the closest relationship we've ever known.

The time and closeness we share with a spouse can far outweigh the time and closeness we've ever experienced with another human. Until our spouse, most of us have never shared a bed with another person since childhood. Waking up every day sharing your dreams and goals and believing that these would be shared forever. To sever that connection, to suddenly be alone with ourselves, we are left alone to mourn the loss of a life partner and all of the dreams, comforts, and beliefs we'd held within them. It doesn't matter if you were the initiator or the opposing force, the pains of grief are heavy. And it hurts. It hurts deeply. And it hurts all around. There's the pain of someone you love so deeply letting you know that they are ready to move forward along on their journey without *you*, and there's the equally heartbreaking pain of having to let someone you love deeply know that you are ready to move forward along on our journey without *them*. The pain of separation runs deep.

The journey through the dark night of divorce is a spiritual, emotional and physical journey. You will experience very visceral responses of the body to the pain of grief, like nausea and sickness in the stomach, physical pains in the heart and left shoulder (heart side) pain that doesn't let up even with surgery. You'll experience migraines, difficulty sleeping and eating, feelings of depression, and uncontrollable tears that triggered at the most seemingly random moments. You will feel a deep raw void at the center of your heart. Confusion.

You may feel guided to change your physical appearance as a part of your healing process. Cutting or coloring the hair, piercing or tattooing the body, embracing a new physical fitness regimen... Treat and take care of yourself throughout the grieving and healing process of separation. Allow a new you to rebirth.

Find ways and tools to bring comfort and healing to your heart, body and soul throughout your period of separation (See Chapter

Nine -Tools to Support the Heart Through Transition). If you are suffering from physical pain that won't let up, consider seeing a spiritual or energetic healer, an acupuncturist or other holistic modality that can work with the subtle layers of the energetic body. These pains run *deep*.

Love knows not its own depth,
until the hour of separation.
KHALIL GIBRAN

9

SURRENDER & REBIRTH

The Dark Night of the Soul

> Time to go into the dark
> where the night has eyes
> to recognize its own.
> There you can be sure
> you are not beyond love.
> The dark will be your womb tonight.
>
> DAVID WHYTE, *SWEET DARKNESS*

These beautiful words by the poet David Whyte describe the Darkness as a womb. Within this dark womb we are at rest, incubating, growing, and awaiting rebirth. The "Dark Night of the Soul" is a concept believed to originally be coined in 16th century by Roman Catholic poet St. John of the cross in his poem titled "The Dark Night". In Roman Catholic and several other mystical traditions, "The Dark Night" is a term used to describe a spiritual crisis in the journey toward union with God. Moving through the "Dark Night of the Soul" is moving from a period of death of the ego or former perceived self, through darkness and into rebirth. It parallels the experience of moving across that Battlefield of Change and battling those Seven Demons of Change as you transition from the old Self across the field to the new liberated Self. This 'period' of darkness is very common to the 'space' of darkness that we fall into when we experience feelings of depression. I have been guided by Spirit with some clients to share that depression is not a lasting condition, but rather it is an emotional state, or a feeling. The emotions and feelings of depression are a calling of the soul for rest, observation and release. Here in contrast to the Dark Night, I explain depression as a space. It is a space that we can fall into and climb out of. It is not a terminal condition but can often be experienced as a chronic condition. The symptoms, feelings, expressions and needs of one walking through the period of their own Dark Night is very similar to the symptoms, feelings, expressions and needs of one whom has fallen into the dark 'space' of depression. The main differentiation between the two is time and control. With depression, you will have control over how long you are there, if depression is a hole you've fallen into, you will be able to crawl or seek help out of it. With the walk through the Dark Night, imagine yourself as Frodo in the Lord of the Rings walking through the Black Lands of Mordor. You can't climb out, your only option is to continue walking forward and through it to reach a brighter place.

Both depression and the Dark Night are brought on by actual loss and the perceptions of loss. (See Chapter 1 section on Illusion of Loss for more.) We've lost a loved one, we've lost our innocence, our Self, we've lost all of our money and resources, we've lost our job. These perceived losses trigger the feelings of depression, and they trigger the walk through the "Dark Night of the Soul." It is crucial to balance our walk through with periods of rest, but when we rest too long in the Dark Night, we feel overcome with depression, we fall into the dark space below, and it is much more difficult to climb out. You'll know it's been too long when you feel overcome by it. This is when traditionally, we reach out to the Divine. If you find yourself overcome with depression, seek professional help, but also begin to connect into the Divine on your own. Whether that be God, Universe, Source, the angelic realms or other source of light, all you have to do is reach out. Help will almost immediately show up for you.

Small steps toward the light will bring you out onto the other side and birth a new You. In your world, these small steps could be going outside for five minutes, reading something empowering, journaling and writing, or seeing a reputable healer. Listen to your internal guidance system and follow each tiny step as it comes. You are constantly being divinely guided. Pause and tune inward to those subtle but powerfully loving voices. These voices are here to guide you forward through your Dark Night.

Symptoms, feelings, expressions of someone navigating depression or the "Dark Night of the Soul":

- Deep feelings of sadness and/or despair
- Questioning life and your purpose here
- Feelings of unworthiness
- Feeling cursed or "condemned" to a life of suffering
- Feelings of emptiness
- Feeling fatigued, weak, tired, powerless and hopeless

Needs of someone navigating depression or the "Dark Night of the Soul":

- A sense of purpose
- Clarity on what excites them
- A sense of home
- Sunlight and fresh air
- A strong network of support

At the end of your walk through the Dark Night, you will emerge a beautiful butterfly warrior, having allowed for the old ego to go to rest and freed yourself of past limitations, beliefs, unhealthy habits and relationships. You will have made it completely across that battlefield. You will have fully manifested into alignment with your Highest Self.

Support & Acceptance of Help

Love is a hero's journey, and the hero's
journey is a noble but difficult path.

MARIANNE WILLIAMSON

ONE of my favorite parallels to the "Dark Night of the Soul" and
the walk across the Battlefield of Change is the Hero's Journey.
The Hero's Journey is a template in comparative mythology of sev-
enteen stages along one's journey of 'life' popularized by Joseph
Campbell, a student of Jung. If you're a fan of *Lord of the Rings,
Harry Potter, or Star Wars,* you'll easily recognize the pattern and
stages of the Hero's Journey. The 17 stages have been studied, orga-
nized and simplified in a number of ways, including through division into three "acts" or parts:

- Departure and/or Separation
- Initiation
- Return

In the departure part of the narrative, the hero lives in
the ordinary world and receives a call for adventure. The
hero is reluctant to follow the call, but is guided by a men-
tor figure. As we move through relationship change, this
is where we begin to feel those stirrings or see the signs
and visions giving us small glimpses into the possibilities.

The initiation section begins with the hero then walking across the threshold into the unknown toward a 'new world', where they face tasks or trials, partially alone and partially with the assistance of helpers.

While alone, the hero reaches "the innermost cave" or the central crisis of his adventure, where he/she faces the main obstacle or enemy, and must summon the assistance of the spiritual, supernatural, or non-physical realm. Once they conquer their enemy and collect a reward, they return home to the ordinary world.

Making it completely across the Battlefield of Change, and through the "Dark Night of the Soul", you will need your strong network of worldly and otherworldly support. Phases of your walk will need to be completed alone, just as any other hero in the Hero's Journey. However there will be times when you absolutely must accept the loving support of others along the way. Again, I say, please know that allowing others to help you is nourishing their need for purpose. Giving and receiving is a gift to others and can take many forms. My client Lana once shared the story of her life-saving kidney donation. A single hardworking woman who'd never had children of her own, she very much needed to feel that she'd offered a service to humanity. As we looked into the energy surrounding this earth angel, we saw that her ability to GIVE an organ of her own body to save the life of another, had come in a time in her life when what she needed the most was to be of service. After giving her kidney, she felt a sense of fulfillment she'd been seeking for decades.

Coming into your time of transition often falls at a synchronous time when someone else in your life is going to need to be of service. It is likely a karmic debt embedded deep within the two of your souls' evolutions. Trust that the help you need will step in in perfect timing. Your job is going to be to accept the offer. We naturally want to know, when/how/who this will be, but the lesson here is for you to remain open to receiving. If you are open, you will know and feel the offering when it comes. When I came into my period of transition following my divorce, I was in need of a safe place to live and have my children part-time until I could afford a place of my own. In that exact time, a colleague of mine had children leaving home for college. She had just enough space to house myself and my three children and made an incredible offer for us to stay until we could be on our own. I was reluctant. I'd been self-sufficient from a very young age, working since age 14, and had never relied on someone for this degree of assistance in my adult life. I was afraid we'd disrupt their structure. I was afraid I couldn't repay her. She assured me that she needed us just as much as we needed her.

Over those months living together we laughed, cried, and celebrated many milestones. We supported each other through relationship troubles and lifted one another up. She was an earth angel for me. One day we sat over a glass of wine sharing stories of past life regressions. I shared how on a recent past life regression I saw myself as a young orphan girl in a European brothel. I cleaned and cared for the home doing small chores and one day an older gentleman came in and requested 'me' the young orphan girl. The mistress of the house obliged and my innocence was taken away. As I shared my account of this past life experience, my earth angel roommate recalled a past life reading she'd had years ago where she'd been a mistress of the house in a European brothel. She remembered the woman describing her as mean spirited and corrupt. We both wondered, if in fact she were the mistress of the house during my past life experience as the young orphan girl. Within my core, I believed that we had been brought together in this life by fate and that quite possibly our love in this lifetime was the forgiveness, karmic balancing, clearing and healing necessary for both of our souls.

When you come into a time of need, trust that whomever shows up in support is there by fate. This opportunity for them to give and for you to receive is an opportunity for deep soul level karmic balancing.

Detachment, Release & Letting Go

 In order to be free, we must learn how to let go. Release the hurt. Release the fear. Refuse to entertain the old pain.

MARY MANIN MORRISSEY

There will be relationships that end against our will. Whether that be a job layoff, a death or a romantic partner leaving before we're ready to let go. These unexpected partings leave us vulnerable, stunned, unprepared for the blunt force hit to our ego and the raw cold of alone-ness to follow.

The Dana Foundation, a private philanthropic organization committed to advancing brain research shared a statistic in January 2000, that at least 25 percent of homicides in the United States involve spouses, sexual partners, or sexual rivals. Each year, some one million American women are followed and harassed by rejected lovers; 370,000 men are stalked by former partners. Men and women in societies everywhere can experience clinical depression when a love relationship fails; and psychologists say that a significant percentage of those who commit suicide do so because they have been rejected by a beloved.

These statistics show the dire consequences of humans today suffering from inability to detach from relationships. Part of the work we can do to prevent this level of suffering is to practice releasing attachment. We naturally become attached to things that feel good to us and every day we form and reform new and old attachments. Through a constant practice of mindfulness we can witness and observe our attachments and free ourselves from them. When you find yourself with an unhealthy attachment to a past lover, family member, friend, colleague, take some time to observe what it is that you are attached to within them. If you find your mind going to unhealthy places when you think about them, use tools of meditation to gently redirect them. Utilize actual distractions. If the thought of detaching and letting go of them brings up thoughts of hopelessness and/or suicide, seek professional help. Mindfulness is a preventative measure that can be taken to minimize all of the above, especially clinical depression, however sometimes additional support is necessary.

What if the other person is having trouble detaching?

If you are in a relationship with someone who is having trouble detaching, you do have power. If you feel threatened, let those in your close trusted circles know. Lean into them for support. Avoid actual contact with the other individual and begin to connect with them on a soul-level. From a place of power and not of pleading, write them a letter asking (or demanding) that they release themselves from you. Let them know that they are hurting you by holding on. Speak directly to their Higher Self. Take the letter and add power to it by creating a full moon ritual and burning it. By burning it, you are releasing yourself from the repeating story.

9.01 Exercise

INTENTION: Release your Self from detachment

ACTION: Sit quietly and write out all of the things in your life that are currently sources of confusion or discomfort. One by one, determine where you can declare acceptance with each of these. For example, if you have recently experienced the loss of a lover and are confused by the process and their reasons for choosing to leave, then write down what you're confused about. What you thought things would 'look like'. Then declare out loud that you accept that things don't look that way. Declare out loud that you accept their choice to leave.

EFFECT: The declaration of acceptance, like mantra or affirmation, can create a powerful shift in the mindset. Here you can shift from feeling powerless and into honoring free will. You release all attachment to your personal agendas and accept the other person's' free will choices.

Cord Cutting & Release

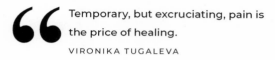

Temporary, but excruciating, pain is
the price of healing.
VIRONIKA TUGALEVA

Cord cutting is a traditional spiritual and energetic practice for freeing ourselves from those who we've formed attachments to or whom still have a grip on us. It runs off of the belief that we can have energetic ties literally binding us to others. In my work, I've seen clients wrapped with what looked like threads, ropes, or leather like cords of light. We work through a series of visualizations to first see and sense the 'cords' themselves, and then we gently allow ourselves to see who or what is on the other end. Sometimes it's a loved one, a family member, parent, or boss. I've even seen an old self holding a leash tightly wound around the neck of the current self. For each individual how we release the cords is unique. Sometimes we unwrap ourselves, sometimes a healer or Shaman like myself will assist, and sometimes we call in the help of our angels and spirit helpers.

Once we've visualized the cutting and uncording process, our final step is to dispose of the cords. This can be through visualizing burying them, tossing them into the sea, giving them back to its sender (rare but if it's someone we trust it is safe), or giving them over to a trusted spirit helper.

The effects of this energetic practice can be felt as a sense of relief and freedom, a sense of excitement for a new start, and they can sometimes be proven effective by a random call or gesture by your former beloved. The Universe has a way of reassuring you that your work in the non-physical is very much affecting the physical, so be open to the signs!

INTENTION: Cut the energetic cords to others that are holding you back

ACTION: Hold the image in your mind of the person you would like to detach from. Begin with just tuning in to their energy. How are they feeling right now? What are they doing? What are they thinking about? Begin to feel into their aura, the light surrounding them, and then into their heart center. Feel into their entire body of light and slowly gradually allow yourself to see ropes, cords, strings binding you to one another. Begin to visualize yourself cutting and freeing any and all from these cords. If you are afraid or feel you need angelic support, call on one of your Spirit helpers or Archangel Michael, the archangel associated with cord cutting and release. He is a beautiful larger-than-life protector, wielding a large gold and silver sword, and acts as a bodyguard of sorts as you step forward and ask for release. Once you feel you've cut and completely uncorded yourself, gather up the ties, and imagine in your mind taking them to a sacred place to release and dispose of them for good. You may choose to burn them, toss them over a cliff and into a body of water or bury them, do whatever you feel guided.

Journaling any thoughts, feelings, fears, sensations that come up for you will help to further process this detachment.

EFFECT: Cord Cutting and Release practices can help you to emotionally and energetically free yourself from unhealthy attachments that are holding you back from thriving in your lives. Trust that although it may feel 'unreal' to you if you are new to soul level communication, your soul is genuinely interacting with that of the other person.

9.02 Exercise

The Gifts of Grief

> When you part from your friend, you grieve
> not; for that which you love most in him
> may be clearer in his absence, as the
> mountain to the climber is clearer
> from the plain.
>
> KHALIL GIBRAN, *THE PROPHET*

Following any undesired separation you will experience grief. Grief can come in waves, unexpected stings, or excruciating pain and leave us feeling debilitated. During any loss or separation, it is imperative that you allow yourself a period to be with this pain, and the only guide for when it's 'time' to come out of it, will be your own heart. Others around you, loved ones, may tell you that you need to get over it or that you need to move on, but your soul will know when it's ready. There is no universal time limit on grief. But when you are ready to move through those waves of pain and seek solace, you will find unexpected gifts.

Catrina came to me for a reading and healing session weeks after the tragic loss of her 25-year-old fiancée, Mark to suicide. His spirit came through quickly and lovingly with supportive and helpful messages to guide her through her grief. He shared incredible details like where he left cash in his car, detailed his Greaser costume that he wore on their last Halloween night and how much fun he'd had. His happy memories brought unexpected gifts of light and laughter in her period of grief. He shared repeated validations to reassure Catrina that he would always be there with her. In session, he showed me a vision of her seven years in the future with children of her own and said that even then he would be there, and that her youngest would provide validation of seeing him. Catrina and I parted ways for a while and six months later she returned to see me. I was in complete awe at how bright she shined after what felt to be such a short time!

During her period of grief Catrina had spent time finding her Self again. She shared with me that at times she felt bad for feeling so alive and so much her Self again. She had loved Mark deeply and still softly grieved his loss, but she shared with me her realization that often times in relationships, we become so intertwined with our partner that we lose track of who we truly are. In her grief and separation, Catrina was gifted with a blanket of time to be with her Self and explore her deepest desires. Other relationships in her life healed and flourished. These did not happen at the cost of the loss, but they happened guided by Spirit in support of her need for healing following the loss. Often times following one loss of a relationship, other relationships are gently and miraculously ushered in to support the heart.

tools to support the heart through grief

In my own grief and in my years of channeling supportive messages from Spirit for others in grief, I've witnessed and gathered a Medicine Wheel of gentle yet powerful tools for navigating grief. Here are some tools that I've found supportive of the heart during grief:

- Music
- Writing & Journaling
- Meditation
- Writing Letters

- Herbal Remedies & Supplements
- Oracle Cards
- Crystals
- A Support Network
- Taking Time for Yourself
- Prayer

music

SOUND and music carries powerful vibrations and frequencies that can literally penetrate through your own energetic body and shift your energy. It can raise your frequency, your vibe. You can find a song to match and support or counter any feelings you're navigating. If you need to sit with the sadness, listen to music that connects you in with the feelings that you are experiencing. If you are needing to escape the sadness, find sound and music that can subtly take you away. Either melodically or with lyric... Here's a little secret to the magic of music... It actually changes our brain chemistry! Music has the power to trigger the release of the same chemicals that are triggered by love and happiness as well as the contrasting sadness and depression. Ask yourself how you would like to feel and then look for music that can take you to those feelings. Do you need to sit with anger? Find some fierce angry music (I love Bishop Briggs, Pink and Demi Lovato for this). Do you need to feel like a strong woman? Try country music from Shania Twain, or power hits from Beyoncé. Allow for the chemical transformation to unfold. When I was moving through my separation, I came across Emeli Sande's deluxe album Long Live the Angels. It told a story of pain and rebirth in "Selah", begging for Divine help with rebuilding the self in the song "Sweet Architect" and coming full circle toward hope and optimism in the end with "Somebody".

This album moved me through sadness, empowerment, hopefulness and newfound love in myself. Find music that helps you move through the emotions of this transition.

writing & journaling

THIS BOOK came of a combination of my own seeking and healing, journaling my own process, and supporting hundreds of others through similar and different transitions of their own. There's no right or wrong when writing, however there is the potential to process old and toxic stories, to channel healing messages and clarity from within, to free yourself and there is also the potential to hold yourself stuck in the same old toxic stories. When you write be mindful of where the writing is carrying you and if it doesn't feel like to a place of power and healing, then redirect or ask the Divine for help with using writing in your healing process. Whether it be journaling, book writing, creative writing, blogging or scribbling... Spirit will speak to you and through you when you write. God, your Higher Self, your angels and guides, they all surround you when you create the quiet space to write or meditate.

meditation

MEDITATION is the practice of taking time to think deeply or clear or focus your mind for a period of time. It can be done in silence or with sound. It can be done for religious or spiritual purposes or as a method of relaxation. When working to process grief and the difficult emotions of separation, take time regularly to experience and observe, through meditation, the emotions that are arising within you. If you've never meditated before, take a class or find a guided meditation via YouTube or a meditation app like Insight Timer or the Calm app. Meditation will be an opportunity for you to process deep emotions, clear the mind and take a momentary respite from the stress and pain of this transition.

writing letters

WRITING letters to our friends, family, former colleagues and ex loves can help us release and shift toxic energy. Write a letter expressing any of the negative feelings, emotions that come up for you when you think of this individual or group and make whatever request or plea you need to release you from that energy. Rather than sharing the letter with them, consider performing a release ritual and burning it with a new or full moon.

herbal remedies & supplements

PLANTS, flowers and herbs are beautiful supportive helping spirits, available to support us in many ways spiritually, emotionally and physically. Herbs to support the heart through grief such as hawthorn, lavender, rose, and lemon balm can be found in most health food stores as tinctures, teas, balms, and in supplemental form. Listen to your inner guidance and/or see a local herbalist if you're feeling guided to the herbs in your healing journey.

oracle cards

ORACLE cards differ from tarot cards in that they are much simpler, average 40-50 cards per deck (as opposed to the 78 card tarot) and come in many different themes and artistic designs for all interests from angels to fairies to unicorns to animals to astrology. I encourage everyone to have a deck of oracle cards to support their connection with Spirit in the more difficult times. Pulling just the right card can guide and encourage you in those moments when you need to feel supported and trusting that you are moving in the right direction. The cards can direct you in what activities you will benefit from dedicating time and energy to, and provide insight into the energy surrounding your situation at various times.

crystals

I WORK with healing stones, minerals and crystals every day. They are helping spirits of the earth. Just as salt and magnesium carry benefits when ingested, other forms of sediment can support us vibrationally and energetically. All stones carry a signature vibrational frequency that can resonate, balance and effect your own frequency. For all of the difficult emotions that you are processing through your transition, there is a crystal to support you. Rose quartz and amethyst are stones that will help to soften your heart and redirect your loving attention inward. Pyrite will help with freeing you from the thoughts and fears of others, red jasper will provide strength, empowerment and courage through your more difficult days. A fierce stone of integrity and courage, Tiger's Eye is highly beneficial for resolving internal battles, issues of self-criticism and low self-worth. Healing stones and crystals can be purchased at local lapidaries and gem shops, metaphysical stores, mind body spirit fairs and festivals, and some wellness centers. You can find them as loose stones to carry in your purse or pocket, wear them as jewelry, or mindfully place them around the home, near the bed, on your altar. You will find many benefits and magic when inviting the crystals into your life.

a support network

Moving through transition you will likely want to be alone a lot. And that is okay. But there will come times when you need and desire to be with others. Lean into your network of family and friends. Clarify your needs: If you need the support of your family and friends but prefer quiet support let them know. If you don't have a solid support network of friends and family, find a grief support group at your local church or therapists' office or a free local support group like Alcoholics Anonymous (AA), Codependents Anonymous (CoDA), or Cognitive Behavioral Therapy Group (CBT). Everyone has a support network, even if you haven't discovered it yet.

taking time for yourself

Engage in quiet activities that are just for you. Go for a walk on the beach or in the woods, sit beside a body of water. Surf. Run. Climb. Yoga. Visit the spa and sit in the steam room. Challenge yourself to try new activities you've never done before or always wanted to try. Getting out and taking time for yourself you will be creating space for the Universe to work more miracles on your behalf. You will find synchronous encounters, helpful people and resources, light.

prayer

CONNECT with your Higher Power and Spirit team and *ask for help*. Ask for help in softening the pain for you. And for others involved. Pray for help with words. With expression of your emotions. Pray for guidance and reassurance and signs that you're making the right decisions. Spirit never fails us and WILL deliver you clear signs each step of the way.

10

ALONE-NESS
SELF-REALIZATION

Suffering & Self-Realization

When I am weak, then I am strong.
2 CORINTHIANS 12

After losing my Mom and questioning God's purpose of suffering, I spent some time in study, prayer and meditation to find understanding into the condition. In addition to the beautiful messages Spirit shared with me regarding the role suffering played in my mother's story and those intertwined within hers, I've found that suffering plays an important role in nearly all religions on the journey to spiritual advancement.

Hinduism holds that suffering follows naturally from personal choices and/or negative behaviors in one's current life or through karma associated with a past life. It teaches that one must accept suffering as a just consequence and as an opportunity for spiritual progress. Thus the soul or true self can come to manifest itself within the person, who then achieves liberation (referred to as 'moksha' in Hinduism).

Christianity teaches that suffering is to be viewed as a positive experience in the climb toward achieving a higher meaning of life, such as Jesus suffering for the lives of other people and later coming to high priesthood in Heaven where He can support and guide us down here on earth. Christianity teaches that suffering is the time to lean into faith find God.

Buddhism teaches within The Four Noble Truths the concept of *dukkha*, a term often translated as suffering. It outlines the nature of suffering, its cause, its cessation, and the way leading to its cessation in Buddhism's the Eightfold Path. Buddhism considers liberation from *dukkha* and the practice of compassion (*karuna*) as basic for leading a holy life and attaining nirvana.

The *sutras*, Buddhist religious texts, teaches of The Four Noble Truths of suffering. The noble truth of the nature of suffering: birth as suffering, aging as suffering, illness as suffering, death as suffering; union with what is displeasing as suffering; separation from what is pleasing as suffering.

The four truths represent the awakening and liberation of the Buddha.

Following any period of suffering comes liberation—it is the natural order. No matter the duration of the suffering. We have free will and as co-creators of our destiny we can bring in the light of liberation at whatever time we choose. Whether we're battling addiction, abuse, neglect, illness within ourselves or in relationship with another, we can exercise our rights to free will to bring ourselves closer to that light. By setting the intention to be freed of our suffering, we begin our walk out onto that Battlefield of Relationship Transition toward liberation.

We are liberated from each period of suffering we were destined to learn from, we are liberated from whatever karma we needed to balance, we are liberated from the beliefs we hold in our reliance on another for survival, we are liberated from codependency.

As the Buddha found, in releasing ourselves from codependency and attachment, we are gifted with a moment of quiet and alone time with the Self. There are beautiful gifts to be found in the quiet solitude of alone-ness that follows leaving relationships. In many traditions, religions, and schools of thought there are beliefs surrounding 'Self-Realization' or 'Self-Actualization' as it is called in traditional psychology. This is the moment of realizing who we truly are. Occurring somewhere in the transitional space between those moments of dependency and liberation. In that space we realize, we remember, and we recognize who we truly are.

Uncovering Your Inner Buddha Self

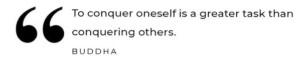

To conquer oneself is a greater task than
conquering others.

BUDDHA

It is in this transitional space of finding joy and purpose within
our Self that we find a new or revived sense of joy and purpose
to share with the world. We come into a new phase of being. We
discover a new version of our Self. We create a new version of our
Self. This period of discovery and creation is to be honored and
celebrated as a pre-destined pivotal point in your journey. In all
of the pain and anguish that you've encountered on that stormy
Battlefield of Relationship Transition, there is such beautiful light
on the horizon as a new enlightened you emerges.

I like to imagine that at the end of transition we emerge as our
"Buddha Self". One who is awake and liberated. Embracing a state
of complete liberation, enlightenment, highest happiness, bliss,
fearlessness, freedom. You've slayed those Demons of Change with
wisdom, compassion, true power, and love. You have reached your
"Nirvana."

10.01 Exercise

INTENTION: Set your own definition and intention for Nirvana

ACTION: List all of the qualities of what "Nirvana" looks like for you? How would you feel at the start and end of each day? How would you flow through your day? How would you relate to others, friends, family, and your children?

EFFECT: Once you have a clear picture of what Nirvana means for you, you can attain it!

Going Forward Alone

 What the superior man seeks is in
himself; what the small man seeks
is in others.
CONFUCIUS

Each time we leave a relationship, we are gifted with an opportunity to be with our Selves again. This can be scary when you've
been in a long term committed relationship. Whether it's a loss
to death, a job loss, a divorce or any other, separation frees us up
to reconnect with our Self. For many, this can be like the opening scene in the movie *Home Alone* when young Macaulay Culkin
wakes up to find that his family has accidentally left him home
alone. That infamous panic scene that quickly shifts into him cele-
brating his independence. Leaving relationships our emotional experience is very much like a swinging pendulum moving between
fear, depression and loneliness to freedom, euphoria and peace.

We are social beings and find joy and purpose in partnerships
and groups. So when we come to our moment of being alone we
can find ourselves face to face with that Demon of Fear. After we
lose a job, we feel the need to search and jump right into another
because we fear we won't have money or purpose. We end a relationship and we fear that we may never find another. Or worse, we
leave a relationship and we fear being alone with our Selves.

Over the years of teaching kids and teens, I've found them to be some of our greatest teachers on the pleasures of being alone. I once asked a group of teens what do they do when they feel lonely. And they individually answered back things like "go outside and do something I like to do," "think about things that make me feel good," and "listen to music and read." I asked them to share about someone in their lives who seems to be lonely and why they believe that they're lonely. They answered back: "{he} just paces around the house like he doesn't know what to do," "{She's} a teacher and that's all she does. She teaches and then after work she doesn't do anything that's for her." "{She} isolates herself and doesn't seem happy."

For my teen group, being alone was either a space to rest in, or a cue to go do something you enjoy. It wasn't a space to sulk or fear or despise. Somewhere post adolescence after we've come to value and sometimes depend on friendships and social circles, we develop a fear of being alone. Many of us need to learn to value our relationships without depending on them. Therefore for so many, we come into a way of being in which we forget the value of our own company. How can anyone else enjoy your company if you yourself don't?

There are many conditional factors that prohibit us from cultivating a solid loving relationship with our Selves, like being taught that it's wrong to be 'selfish' and right to care more for others than ourselves. Subsequently, many people leave relationships having attached much of their own value to another person, place or organization and in the absence of it, experiencing an uncomfortable moment of low self-worth, loss of sense of Self, suffering feelings of emptiness and loneliness.

Loneliness or Solitude

You cannot be lonely if you like the person you're alone with.

WAYNE DYER

LONELINESS is defined as a state of sadness in the fact of being isolated or without a companion. Emptiness is the feeling of lacking something or containing nothing. Emptiness is the internal lack, loneliness the external.

If you are feeling lonely, what type of external companionship are you seeking?

There are times in our lives that we will be without romantic companionship, without platonic companionship, without familial companionship. Even those who are married for decades still have times within those relationships where they lack romantic companionship. During these times where we lack a particular form of companionship, we have an opportunity to explore the other realms of relating and companionship. If you are without a romantic partner, take this time to honor family. If you are without family, take this time to honor friendships. Lack is an opportunity for observation, reflection, and reception. In your loneliness... take your time to slow down and observe your surroundings. Reflect on what you're seeking. Be receptive to what's on offer. This doesn't mean to settle for just any attention, but as you begin to allow yourself to gratefully receive attention, you become more and more open to receiving more specifically what you're seeking.

My client Brittany was opening her heart up to new romantic relationships but felt she wasn't meeting anyone. I was shown an image of her at a local coffee shop or juice bar ordering her drink and immediately walking out. Spirit asked her to please slow down. Sit down and have her drink. There was a man just across the room with his eye on her, and in her hurry she hadn't even noticed. When you're seeking companionship, explore being mindful in each moment. Observing your surroundings, moving slowly, enjoying your time with yourself, being open and receptive to interactions with those around you.

Slow down.

I use the word alone-ness as a transformative condition to the lower vibrational 'lonely-ness.' When I think of alone-ness, I think of solitude and I think of a choice. A choice to be alone and a celebration of time and space with my Self.

During periods of alone-ness, intentional isolation, and solitude when we have left relationships with others, we are gifted with a moment to reconnect and be with our Selves. This is an opportunity for further personal growth and evolution, and most importantly it is an opportunity to find peace within.

10.02 Exercise

INTENTION: Find the gifts in your time of solitude

ACTION: Write a list of all of the things that you would love to do in your spare time or on a day or week off. Have fun.

- Travel
- Redecorate your house
- Plan a party
- Paint, sculpt, make jewelry, do something creative
- Garden
- Go on a retreat
- Go back to school
- Take an online course
- Cook
- Go for a hike, or run, or walk

EFFECT: Post this list somewhere easily accessible that you can refer back to again and again. In those moments when you are feeling lonely and don't know what to do with your Self, these activities will be your medicine.

Emptiness or Contentment

> Through births and deaths,
> Haunting oceans of emptiness,
> She solely walks with
> Universal falling stars.
>
> PHEN WESTON

Remember my client Hannah who explained that she had this feeling of emptiness come over her during a lunch date with her husband? After connecting in with Spirit and asking the question of what triggered the sinking sensation of emptiness that she described, Spirit shared one word 'contentment' and the message that in that moment, she had a flash thought of 'Is this it?'. I guided Hannah through a beautiful meditation in which she came to lie beside a still pond. The pond was full, yet it was still, with no ripples, no waves, no sound. "Your life right now is like this pond" Spirit said. There was nothing wrong, in fact everything was right. My client came out of that meditation feeling very at peace and realizing that the sensation of emptiness and lack of fulfillment was really just a beautiful moment of stillness. Her "pond of life" was not empty, it was filled with the recent completion of a doctorate degree, a fulfilling career, a loving and supportive husband, a recently transformed healthy body and so much more.

When you find yourself feeling empty, deep dive into your own pond with these questions:

What is my pond filled with RIGHT now? What do I have to

celebrate in my life? What have I recently completed? What trans-formation have I recently undergone? What am I content with?

Wholeness

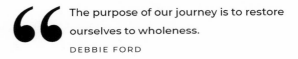

> The purpose of our journey is to restore
> ourselves to wholeness.
> DEBBIE FORD

In shamanic tradition, there is a belief that you have multiple Selves within you. You've held and left relationship with each of these Selves throughout the course of your life. They are sometimes left behind by choice and sometimes unwillingly. Sometimes they are shed naturally and sometimes they are stolen from us. A large part of my work as Shaman is helping others to heal, retrieve and reconnect with lost parts of the Self. Knowing and reconnecting with your Self at key pre- and post-trauma events supports you in reconnecting with the gifts, talents and passions that have been seeded within you since before you even came to earth. In soul retrieval work we journey back through time to reconnect and reclaim your lost soul parts to support a new sense of connected-ness and whole-ness within you.

I often marvel at how much my adult Self has evolved from my college-aged Self from my teenage Self. As a teenager I was spiritual, stylish, sure of myself, deeply creative and a passionate writer. In college I swapped in my fashionable wardrobe for Ohio State University hoodies and yoga pants and left the fine arts program to follow the path of architecture. I fed the spiritual tugging in my heart by attending in depth yoga courses, philosophy and Anthropology and fed my passion for writing by enrolling in extra-curricular women's writers courses. Fresh out of college I was married with my first child and committed to a well-paying position with a top international architecture firm in Washington DC. Here I swapped in my hoodies and yoga pants for a professional uniform of dark slacks and casual tops. I no longer fed my passions for writing and spiritual study. I slowly began to lose my Self. It was my 17-year-old self that I retrieved during my healing process to empower and guide me forward in feeding and nourishing those hungers within myself, catapulting me into my purpose as a writer, healer, teacher. In much of my work with others, it is the 17-year-old Self that does the same for them.

Are you ready to recover and reconnect with lost parts of your Self and catapult forward in your purpose and passions? Are you seeking to find your Self as you navigate leaving relationships in your present? Let's reconnect with your 17-year-old self and any others that are ready to support you.

INTENTION: Journal exercise to retrieve your own past selves

ACTION: Approach this exercise as a sacred journaling session. Light incense, sage or candle, play light music, get comfy. Say a prayer for peace and healing. Then do the following:

1. In your journal write down five ages that pop into your mind.
2. For each age listed sit for a few minutes in meditation. What qualities did you possess at this age? What were your gifts? Strengths? How would you describe yourself at this age?
3. As you think about yourself at an age, allow for a specific memory to come into your awareness. Begin writing whatever comes to you, no matter how mundane. Writing every single detail that comes. In my soul retrieval work with clients, it is often the clothing we wear, the music we listen to, the way we styled our hair, the activities we participated in... That reconnect us with our former Selves. Notice how these things made you feel. Write it down.
4. After completing all five ages, take a look at your entire list. Determine what parts of yourself you would like to bring forward into your now. Visualize yourself gathering up these qualities like small balls of light into a basket. If you feel guided to gather up the entire self, visualize looking her/him into the eyes and asking them to come forward with you. Letting them know that you need them.
5. Complete the retrieval process with large breaths for each soul part or quality brought back, imagining breathing it back into your own heart. Take a moment of gratitude and allow all parts to settle into place.

EFFECT: Reconnecting with lost and forgotten parts of ourselves helps us to feel more whole, more centered and more grounded in our Self. Often times as a result of retrieving and remembering lost parts, we are able to make important life decisions with greater clarity, gain confidence to move forward and feel a stronger sense of knowing who we are.

11

LEAVING WITH LOVE

Loving Your Self

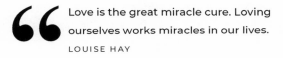

Love is the great miracle cure. Loving
ourselves works miracles in our lives.
LOUISE HAY

When I came into my period of alone-ness after my divorce, I too
rode that swinging pendulum of emotion. I moved between feelings of loneliness and feelings of complete liberation. From eating
ice cream in bed for dinner while watching movies to late night
binge watching YouTube Astrology videos seeking some form of
prediction to when my alone-period would end to having cry fests
and pity parties sulking at the empty half of my king-size bed—I
was a mess. I found pride in myself when I would get outside of
the house. My work was my savior. Being of service, feeling pur-
poseful, genuinely helping others, was my greatest source of motivation. The loving voices of my Spirit guides in my mind, whis-
pering to me to go to the sea... I would listen and heed that advice.
I would sit in meditation in front of the water, and feel that immense love of God, Universe, Gaia...

I set an intention to be my own best date. If there was a restau-
rant I wanted to try, I went. If I wanted to catch live music, I went.
If I wanted to go to a festival or show, I went. If I wanted to drive
10 hours to the mountains for a weekend... I went! I told myself,
no limits! I would ask my angels and helping Spirits to make each

experience magical. And without fail, each experience would be filled with synchronicity, positivity and fun. In what could have been a dark void in being alone, there was love, light and comfort in the outside world. I momentarily abandoned my perceived 'need' for romantic love and gently allowed myself to receive all other forms of love with deep gratitude.

I found love in my children, my family, my team, my clients, and my friends.

I found love in my Self.

The more I dated my Self, the more I fell in love with her. In the year following my divorce, I created exercises and practices that lead to my first Self-Love Challenge. I invited clients and participants to engage with me and share in a month of self-loving exercises, journaling prompts and assignments. I shared my collection of practical and spiritual tools for self-love.

I found such inspiration in my clients' and my own learnings from the Self-Love Challenge, I continued another year. In the second round, I had a participant standout and share that she'd considered leaving the challenge after the mirror exercise in 'Body Love,' the most difficult challenge of them all. In this exercise I invite participants to stand in front of the mirror nude or in their underwear daily (yes, that means no clothing). First, we stand in observation and we tell the figure staring back at us that we love her/him. The same woman who considered leaving, shared that she reached out to several friends and colleagues and asked if they thought they'd be able to look at themselves in the mirror and love that reflection and many (if not all) said no. Many of us have not been conditioned to love ourselves and our bodies and this particular challenge is an effort to reprogram our entire system of body-love AND self-love.

In taking a period of time to date and explore loving our Selves we learn our hang-ups and insecurities. As we work through them we are doing our future selves a great service in releasing these blocks before we enter into another relationship. Whether it's a working relationship or a love relationship, we benefit greatly from entering into it without the weight of past insecurities.

If we can't love the reflection in the mirror, then how can we expect another to?

We *can* expect them to. And they might. But we won't be positioned to wholeheartedly RECEIVE that love.

The act of looking in the mirror is a play between giving and receiving. When we look in the mirror in these self-love exercises, we are practicing looking, *giving attention* and reflecting, *receiving attention*. It is a practice. I place this practice at the beginning of the month-long challenge because I know that it is difficult. Just as with any new skill we desire to cultivate, the practice of self-love takes dedication, perseverance and 'practice.' The more you practice something, the more natural it will become to you.

If we desire to receive love, then there is no choice but to love that reflection. In all Truth, each relationship and each person we love, no matter how glorious or how painful... Is a reflection of our Self.

INTENTION: Mirror exercise to connect in to deeper love for your Self.

ACTION: Find a mirror that you can sit comfortably in front of for 10-15 minutes. 30 if you're feeling adventurous. Light a candle and have a journal or voice recorder nearby.

With the lights dimmed, sit and begin to connect in with your breathing. Center yourself, connect in with your body and heart center by simply breathing deeply and holding the intention to connect in with your Self. Find your eyes in the reflection in the mirror and slowly allow for a specific age to come into your mind. If you hear "6" in your mind, or think of age "14" or see your 38 year old face... Listen and trust and allow your mind and spirit to be guided back to that age. Allow the reflection gazing back at you to become that version of yourself. If you heard "6", then imagine your 6 year old self gazing back at you through that mirror. Feel their energy, their heart, their spirit. What were some of their best qualities? What was wondrous about your Self at that time? What did you love? Who were you? Speak these qualities out loud or record them into your journal.

Feel into your innocence.

Whisper to your Self all of the things that you needed to hear.

Whisper to your Self, "I love you. I will take care of you." And imagine that younger version of You coming through the mirror and embracing you.

Breathe your Self in.

EFFECT: Devoid of the layers of shame, guilt, self loathing and regret that build over the years, you are able to connect in with the innocence and purity of your True Self with greater ease and love them unconditionally.

Goodbye with Love

 Goodbyes are only for those who love
with their eyes. Because for those who
love with heart and soul there is no such
thing as separation.
RUMI

CONGRATULATIONS! You have accomplished so much in working with this book. You've come to understand the truths of impermanence, slayed the Demons of Change, begun to free yourself from resistance, forgiven your Self and those you love, made a plan for moving forward, uncovered your inner Buddha, found gratitude in the lessons learned from the relationship 'teachers' in your life and fallen in love with your Self.

All of our relationships are opportunities for us to come closer to knowing God-love within ourselves and God-love within All. You may call it Universe, Source, Qi, Light... whatever you call it, it is our one true source of love. Endings of relationships can thrust us right into the arms of this one source of love. Whether a loss of a child to independence and adulthood, loss of a family member to heaven, loss of a job to economic downfall, or loss of a lover to another... we have the opportunity to fall right into the arms of *True* love. There is where we find the reflection of peace, acceptance, forgiveness, understanding, compassion, and our true Self. And it is there, in that reflection, that we truly **Leave with Love**.

GLOSSARY

Ascension: the departure from the stress and weight of the excess of energies and choices available to us. It is the upward movement of the Spirit through understanding, grace, and awareness into Higher Consciousness. The International Standard Bible Encyclopedia defines the ascension of Jesus as 'the departure of Christ from Earth into the presence of God'.

Catalyst: a substance that enables a chemical reaction to proceed at a usually faster rate or under different conditions (as at a lower temperature) than otherwise possible. an agent that provokes or speeds significant change or action

Divine: A collective of supportive energy and figures like or of God.

Impermanence: the quality or state of being impermanent. Everything in existence, including living beings, is transient, temporary, comes into being and dissolves. Nothing lasts, and everything decays.

Karma: a belief in the flow of energy from one source to another. As it flows between sources there is a constant striving attempt to be in balance. A balancing between polarities. Those sources can be two people, a person and an entity or cause, or two aspects of one person, the energy flows through intentions, actions, service, and deeds. Traditionally a concept based in Hinduism and Buddhism, the concept of karma is now common course in western culture, language and philosophy. Encyclopedia Britannica defines Karma as a spiritual principle of cause and effect where intent and actions of an individual (cause) influence the future of that individual (effect).

Metamorphosis: the process of transformation from an immature form to a mature adult form

Non-Attachment: A practice of releasing the ego and letting go of people, places, ideas that have a hold on you.

Soul Retrieval: A traditional shamanic practice of journeying through time in deep meditation or trance to retrieve and restore lost parts of the soul.

Spirit: The collective voice of Higher consciousness and being of light. Your own angels, Higher Self, spirit guides, ascended masters.

About the Author

Athena Allread is a writer and practicing shaman in the quaint beach town of Lewes, Delaware. Athena incorporates traditional shamanic techniques such as soul retrieval and shamanic journey into a fusion of past life regression work, intuitive reading and Spirit therapy. She helps individuals navigate and free themselves from mental, emotional, and physical manifestations of grief, trauma, and dis-ease. After navigating loss and divorce Athena is passionate to share her experience and the tools that supported her and hundreds of her clients through her writing. She is co-owner of Lanikai Wellness studio in Milton, Delaware and mother of Lark, Wolf, and Kai. Athena enjoys dancing, writing, meditating with the sea and empowering others to work with their own loving helpers of the Spirit World on their unique journeys toward healing.

Learn more about her and her work at **www.seasideshaman.com**

74579702R00114

Made in the USA
Columbia, SC
12 September 2019